Managing Libraries in Transition

by Jennifer Cargill and Gisela M. Webb

Phoenix • New York
ORYX PRESS
1988

The rare Arabian Oryx is believed to have inspired the myth of the unicorn. This desert antelope became virtually extinct in the early 1960s. At that time several groups of international conservationists arranged to have 9 animals sent to the Phoenix Zoo to be the nucleus of a captive breeding herd. Today the Oryx population is over 500, and herds have been returned to reserves in Israel, Jordan, and Oman.

Copyright © 1988
by Jennifer Cargill and Gisela M. Webb

Published by The Oryx Press
2214 North Central at Encanto
Phoenix, Arizona 85004-1483

Published simultaneously in Canada

Printed and Bound in the United States of America

∞ The paper used in this publication meets the minimum requirements of American National Standard for Information Science—Permanence of Paper for Printed Library Materials, ANSI Z39.48, 1984.

Library of Congress Cataloging-in-Publication Data

Cargill, Jennifer S.
  Managing libraries in transition.

  Bibliography: p.
  Includes index.
  1. Library administration.   2. Library personnel management.   3. Library science—Technological innovations.   I. Webb, Gisela M.   II. Title.
  Z678.C29   1988   025.1   87-24703
  ISBN 0-89774-302-4

Contents

Preface

Libraries are at a critical juncture in their evolution. There is pressure and competition created by technological innovations, networks, user demands, and the increased information requirements of a new age. Other disciplines are also noting the emphasis on and importance of information dissemination and are making their own efforts to take charge of the information world. Auxiliary computer centers are developing rapidly; computer center directors and library directors are seeing their areas of responsibility blur. In some instances computer centers and libraries are being placed under the administrative control of one individual. Whether that "information czar" has a computer or library background has become a sensitive issue.

These changes demand new missions, goals, objectives, organizational structures, services, staffing patterns, employee qualifications, and managerial skills. Today libraries are being forced to examine their very existence and justify the need for their services. In the past they were perceived as information monopolies, intrinsically good and valuable for society, comparable to motherhood and apple pie.

In the 1980s information has become a commodity that the public can access and use without ever entering a library. Libraries, their staffs, and resources can be used through remote access or can be bypassed entirely. Database searching, for example, can be done by the end user without any involvement from a librarian or ever approaching the traditional reference station.

As libraries become increasingly transitional in organizational structure, in mission, in expectations, managing them requires an understanding of the issues that arise and demands development of different skills and different strategies. In addition, library managers must become more aware of, and sensitive to, the changing demands of the library labor force, which is requiring more involvement and benefits from the library profession.

The stresses created by this changing environment are leading to increased staff turnover. Career changes—people moving in and out of the profession—are becoming commonplace. In addition, alternative career paths are opening up for women and shrinking the traditional labor pool for libraries. Some of the best and the brightest librarians are taking advantage of nontraditional professional opportunities, leaving librarianship as a career for the less assertive and more security conscious. Yet, many who are willing to stay in the profession are no longer satisfied with genteel poverty. They demand adequate compensation, intellectually stimulating jobs, promotional opportunities, and participative environments.

Long-established library administrators are for the most part not prepared for and are puzzled by these new staff demands. The managerial techniques they learned are no longer applicable. They grew accustomed to exerting unquestioned authority. They are comfortable with the rigid organizational arrangements they created, where functions were compartmentalized, and authority lines were not crossed. Many of these administrators are in the age range of over 55, approaching the end of their library careers. They have hired and promoted other administrators who share their philosophy and fit into these traditional organizations. Now this managerial group finds the rules of the administrative game changing and their staffs view their styles as static and unacceptable.

These managers often perceive the changes demanded by their staffs or parent organizations as fads which will not last and which should be ignored. They fear that employees will only consider their personal needs in a participative environment and will develop unreasonable expectations which cannot be met. Traditional administrators expect their employees to remain focused on doing their jobs within narrowly defined schedules and guidelines, adhering to an unquestioned work ethic. If these administrators consider themselves benevolent, they most likely leave the emerging work problems unresolved, inappropriate behavior unchallenged, personality clashes festering, and inadequate performance unaddressed. They hope that the organization will return to normal again and life will continue as before.

Managing Libraries in Transition should be especially useful for those administrators who find themselves hired into traditional organizations where changing expectations and environments have been largely ignored. In many cases the previous administrators will have retired after long tenures, leaving with organizational energies at a low point and activities performed in predictable, established patterns.

In other instances, traditional library managers will have left in frustration after the greater environment changed and encouraged a move toward participative management. They probably felt caught between eager staffs and aware superiors, both pushing for administrative changes that they were unable to lead or understand.

It is hoped that this book will also be helpful to those administrators brave enough to initiate changes in their libraries. It is written to add to their understanding of the change process and to give them some practical advice on how to tackle the most common problems encountered. And to those who aspire to higher-level managerial positions but have not yet arrived, we hope to impart some knowledge about the complexities of today's organizations and to inspire them to become change agents within their own organizations, hopefully in cooperation with enlightened administrators.

Introduction

Artists, businesspeople, politicians, visionaries, and other leaders in tune with today's environment sense the coming of a new age. Whether we call it the Space Age, the Information Age, the Third Wave, the Post-Industrial Society, or the Age of Maturity, it appears to be characterized by new lifestyles, value systems, relationships, political alignments, and work environments.

The revolutionary changes taking place today are affecting everybody's lives. Freed from outdated customs, conventions, assumptions, and structures, some people are experiencing renewed bursts of creative energies. These individuals are ready for the challenges of the new civilization and anticipate playing an active part in the re-creation of human relationships and societal institutions. Others despair over the disappearance of tried and true values, life structures, and predictable patterns of living and working. In the past we had the luxury of time to speculate about the future. Today the future threatens to overwhelm us, and we are forced to address the immediate concerns of the present that are confronting us.

During our lifetimes, we've seen more revolutionary developments unveiled than ever before in history. Change has become the only predictable component in our lives. Growing up in a society in which decisions were thrust upon us, we now find ourselves in a world where we are increasingly a part of the decision-making process. For most of us, the work environment is the main place where major adjustments in attitudes, actions, and values are demanded. If we have based our work concepts on a traditional work ethic with hierarchical organizations and centralized authority, the emerging environment may feel uncomfortable and stressful.

THE CHANGING WORK ETHIC

The traditional American work ethic was based on religious and economic values which assumed that work provided the only sure path to eternal salvation and worldly success. Today's work force is motivated by more diverse and individualistic needs. As the nation moved from an agrarian society through industrialization toward an information society, work attitudes and values were challenged and adjusted to incorporate conditions created by the efficiencies of the factory system and technology. Concerns about scarcity and the economic necessity to produce more were replaced by society's search to equitably allocate its products and to handle the effects of excess capacity. As time passed people grew wary in the beliefs that spectacular success was possible through hard work. They adopted more realistic expectations, knowing from experience that Horatio Alger-like success stories are the exception and not the rule.

The latest changes in work values have accelerated because of technological developments. Technology has eliminated many physically demanding, tedious, and unpleasant jobs. Newly created positions in turn often require a better educated work force with more diverse skills or else consist of monotonous and dehumanizing tasks. The work force itself has changed from being homogeneous, mostly male and White, to include a growing percentage of female and minority employees, with different aspirations and value systems.

As pay, benefits, and working conditions have generally increased despite a shortening of the work week, the privilege of having a job has been replaced by the right to have a job. The focus on personal responsibility of job holders has shifted to society's responsibility to provide training and full employment. Despite these improvements, employers today are commonly faced with expressions of work alienation and dissatisfaction such as insubordination and hostility, increased absenteeism and turnover, shoddy workmanship, sabotaging of equipment and products, and alcohol and drug abuse.

Employees everywhere expect that democratic conditions prevalent in their political and social environment are now to be incorporated and practiced in their work lives. Their beliefs have been reinforced during the last two decades as limits have been placed on the use or misuse of authority through political and legal means. Rising educational levels and aspirations prepare them well to articulate questions about institutional policies and goals. Workers insist on exercising their inalienable rights of free speech, dissent, fair and equitable treatment, and due process.

The attitudes of younger workers appear to pose the greatest challenge to institutions. For them the value of work depends on the nature of the job; work is not necessarily considered rewarding on its own. Work is thought to be important only to employees with high-status jobs. If the work ethic shows a decline, the young workers place the responsibility on managers who have created meaningless jobs, worthless products, and impersonal organizations.

Because younger workers regard government and church welfare and help from family and friends as more acceptable than older workers, they are more likely to quit their jobs and experience periods of unemployment. As a result of changing social values during the 1960s, the connections between material well-being, quality of life, job satisfaction, and a strong work ethic seem to have disappeared. Younger employees were raised in an era of affluence, where basic needs have always been met either by parents or by society through governmental programs. These programs range from unemployment compensation, which helps to soften the impact of a job loss, to assistance to industries that can no longer compete with a world marketplace. When younger workers see factories or entire industries shuttered, competition from foreign companies crippling U.S. industries, and leveraged buyouts, they become less expectant of long-term employment in one company.

Management, limited by its own assumptions, did not perceive itself as responsible for helping workers develop the necessary skills to function in a participative role. As a result, frustrations are increasing on both sides. Managers blame employees for wanting authority without responsibility and employees complain about the lack of involvement in decisions that vitally affect their lives.

CHANGES IN MANAGEMENT THEORY

In response to the times and economic conditions, management styles and philosophies have experienced equally significant changes as have work ethics and values. Management theories evolved from studying and fostering organizational concerns for maximum production at the lowest cost to recognizing the importance of human beings as the most important resource in the work place.

Scientific or Classical Management Theory

At the beginning of this century the *scientific* or *classical management theory* was developed by Frederick Winslow Taylor with the focus on technological issues. Taylor proposed that the best way to increase productivity was to improve the methods, techniques, and tools used by the workers. Time and motion studies were developed during that period and people were considered extensions of machines and instruments to be manipulated by their leaders for the best output. Management did not concern itself with the social and psychological dimensions of human beings. Assumptions were that workers had no choice but to adjust to organizations and working conditions.

Leadership was meant to define and set performance criteria for the achievement of organizational goals. Increased production was the result of rational planning and technology. Money was considered the primary motivator of workers and their economic self-interest would be achieved through incentive work plans such as piece rates and mass production techniques.

Administrative Management School

Fostered by Max Weber's writings on the nature of bureaucracies, the *administrative management school* also developed in the early 1900s. Its proponents focused on the responsibilities of middle and upper management levels and emphasized the need for organizational hierarchies, limited spans of control, and rigid communication channels. Horizontal communication between workers was acceptable only if work-related and sanctioned by upper-level management.

Human Relations Movement

The classical management era was replaced by the *human relations movement* during the 1920s and early 1930s. Its ideas and concepts grew out of the famous Hawthorne studies conducted by Elton Mayo at Western Electric's Hawthorne, Illinois plant. He and other researchers discovered by studying the effects of illumination on productivity, that in addition to finding the best technological methods to improve productivity, management needs to pay attention to social and human factors. They argued that the real power centers within an organization were the interpersonal relations that developed within work groups. Management was advised to study human relationships and develop the organization around the workers, taking into consideration their needs, motivations, feelings, and attitudes.

Mayo considered the scientific management view that workers were concerned only with economic self-interest degrading. It denied workers the opportunity to satisfy higher order needs and led to feelings of anxiety, frustration, and anger. He deplored the task-oriented managerial practices he observed, because they made workers feel like unimportant, disconnected victims of their environment. The studies concluded that openness, honesty, and trust facilitate the transfer of information, which is necessary for productive organizations. Money was no longer considered the prime motivator for workers, but was replaced by the existence of supportive human relationships and personal development opportunities. As a result managerial focus shifted from organizational goals to human resource concerns.

Human Resources Management Philosophy

The work of Mayo and other human relations management theorists provided the foundation for the development of the *human resources management philosophy,* which developed after World War II. Some basic concepts proposed include:

1. Work is not distasteful and, in the proper environment, workers will want to do the best possible job.
2. People can be creative in the proper work environment.
3. Workers will assume responsibilities when properly motivated.

Douglas McGregor formulated the now classic Theory X-Theory Y concept during this time. He proposed that managers espouse certain managerial theories based on their underlying assumptions about human nature and human motivation. Theory X managers assume that people are lazy and irresponsible, prefer to be directed, and care most about their safety. They believe that money, fringe benefits, and the threat of punishment are the basic managerial techniques through which workers are controlled. They create highly structured and closely supervised environments.

McGregor believed that this view of human nature was incorrect and that managerial practices based on it were, therefore, counterproductive. He developed an alternative theory of human behavior which assumes that people are basically self-directed and creative, if properly motivated. Management's task is to create the conditions wherein human potential can be released and developed. Self-motivated workers will achieve organizational goals by controlling their own efforts.

McGregor and others recommend that management create organizational climates in which workers have the opportunity to grow as individuals and group members and thereby work to meet their own needs as well as those of the organization.

Managing Today's Organizations

Today's management theories merge the findings and research from previous eras, recognizing that capital, technical, and human resources are important assets that require proper management. Based on current management theory, creating productive opportunities for today's workers is a basic managerial responsibility. Managing with the needs of employees in mind requires knowledge, concern, planning, and empathy. Research has borne out that managers who are cognizant of subordinates' attitudes and needs are more effective supervisors.

What can organizations do to develop the essential skills in managers and workers to achieve an effective partnership between management and employees?

Employees' views of top management affect work attitude more directly than any other factor—more than supervisory management, salary, fringe benefits, job training, coworker relations, and company policies and procedures. Organizational problems often develop because workers perceive managers to be more concerned with their own self-interest than the collective good of the organization. If new organizational climates, with participative work values, are to be created, managers are required to set a good example. Supervisors, for example, exert a much greater influence on subordinates through their personal behavior than through their orders and directives.

Company philosophies about quality, service, pride, cooperation, or punctuality are just words if supervisors disregard them in their actions. When employees have not had a lot of experience in participative decision making, they observe how decisions are made at the top administrative levels and fashion their own behavior accordingly.

To enable an organization to function effectively, it has to have a mission or purpose which justifies its existence. This mission needs to be communicated to all its members to solicit their personal commitment. The organizational structure, the job functions, and individual positions need to be carefully designed and adjusted to support the mission and minimize constraints. Through communication of managerial and worker expectations, a dialog can be developed that helps each member internalize organizational values upon which future joint decision making can be built. The personal commitment to goals and acceptance of responsibility for their achievement can be developed through ever increasing delegation of assignments. It is management's role to provide encouragement after responsibility has been delegated, assist with unanticipated problems, evaluate job performance, and reward effective work behavior.

Commitment to organizational goals increases as staff involvement in their creation increases. Job and organizational redesign efforts need to be used to strengthen personal understanding of how one contributes to an holistic effort. Innovative strategies and behavior must receive special acknowledgment and encouragement. Employee willingness to improve through personal and professional education needs to be consistently rewarded, because today's organizations depend on their employees to anticipate needs and plan for excellence.

Rapid technological innovations have made the obsolescence of knowledge and skills a real issue. Employers and professional organizations are starting to accept their responsibilities in providing opportunities for learning, hoping to motivate their staffs to update their work skills. Continuing education classes, training programs and materials, workshops, sabbaticals, retreats, and job rotations are some of the proliferating tools used to combat outdated information and skills.

While all these actions are valuable and helpful, the motivation to learn and the realization that one's skills are outdated must be personal. Organizations must direct their primary efforts toward strengthening work values and providing opportunities for employees to recognize that their jobs and contributions are vital within a larger social context. Working hard, being productive, being concerned for one's coworkers, having knowledge of the organizational mission, and knowing one's contributions toward its achievements contribute more to job satisfaction than money and status.

Productivity of workers will increase with their assumption of responsibility for the tasks to be performed. Managers must know their employees as individuals, determine what motivates each one, and provide a work environment where they can exercise discretion, make decisions, and become responsible for their output. Management must be aware that what it thinks is often secondary to what the workers think; workers must learn that what the individual thinks is not as important as what the group thinks.

To master the challenges present in today's organization, the efforts of all are required; ideas need to flow from the bottom up while encouragement and respect must come from the top down. Only organizations that foster participation and involvement of all their employees will succeed.

PART I

Changing Organizational Environments

Chapter 1
Laying the Groundwork for Change

An administrator who finds him or herself in a changing organization can expect to experience philosophical differences with some staff and increased stress as he or she begins to use different managerial techniques and approaches to work. The majority of library staff, including the top administrators, may very well be intellectually supportive of the changes. Some, however, will lack the necessary skills to implement new directions and in their anxiety may start to undermine the fledgling attempts to create a new organizational environment.

ORGANIZATIONAL ANALYSIS

Before embarking on radical reorganizations, instituting sweeping changes, and developing new programs for which they thought they were hired to implement, new administrators may be wise to conduct a thorough analysis of the organization itself to gain insights into the prevalent climate. Although some of this investigation should have been done before the position was accepted, one's presence in an organization provides additional opportunities for firsthand observations and access to previously unavailable information sources, which may or may not confirm initial impressions.

Informal talks with all staff members can provide a wealth of information about the history of the organization and its formal and informal leadership. It will be a good idea to alert both superiors and subordinates that changes will not be forthcoming until all staff members have had a chance to discuss their concerns, hopes, and aspirations, and a thorough assessment of the organizational state of the art is completed.

Such an approach will give new administrators some time to look at all aspects of the organization, give the appearance of thoroughness and impartiality, and probably prevent costly mistakes, made in haste, to impress the wrong people.

The manager who takes the time to have private interviews, or "one-to-ones," with all staff will find the results worthwhile. In these conversations, the new manager can relate his or her expectations of staff at all levels, describe his or her managerial style, indicate potential organizational changes as a result of the changing direction of the parent organization, and arrive at an understanding of issues that concern individual staff. These private interviews with staff should be accompanied by formal or informal orientations to the present work flow, policies, and procedures.

The resulting written assessment of the status quo of the organization, once compiled, can be shared with the next administrative level and with selected staff members. The document should include an assessment of strengths and weaknesses of individual staff, an analysis of present policies and procedures, and an indication of where problems exist or potentially will surface.

Undertaking such a study of the organization, whether it be a single department, a division, or the entire organization, requires that the administrator objectively analyze the library and its staff, assess the direction in which the library is presently moving, and attempt to formulate the future. While compiling a "white paper" is not an easy process, it does require the manager to think through issues and articulate his or her own opinion of the organization and its staff. It can serve as the basis for communication between the new managers and their superiors, providing insights into their philosophy, expertise, and human relations skills. Since proposals on how to correct perceived problems are included, goal setting can occur and a new administrator will have a road map to follow at least for the first year.

New administrators in turn can test the commitment of superiors and subordinates toward a change effort with such a document. If, for instance, dysfunctional work areas are identified and documented, but higher administrators or staff discourage the implementation of workable solutions, a new administrator will have to reassess the organizational commitment to change.

After writing a thorough analysis and having its conclusions accepted by the formal and informal organizational leaders, new managers have numerous approaches available to involve staff at all levels to bring about a more participative and humanistic environment. Committees, task forces, quality circles, staff development, training, job enrichment and redesign programs are the most commonly recommended and successfully used techniques.

PARTICIPATION AND ACCOUNTABILITY

Library managers in changing organizations will realize early that staff does not become an effective partner in a participative environment just because management or staff wish it. There will be attempts by many staff members to request the authority to make changes but leave the responsibility with the manager. Embarking on any change implies a risk. While staff will, at first, be happy to take credit if change efforts prove successful, they will not want to take responsibility for changes that fail. New managers need to back up and reassure the few natural risk takers that failure will be acceptable and that risk-taking is part of one's professional responsibility. Some employees, after years of talking about being underutilized and not appreciated for their talents, will become paralyzed when faced with new responsibilities. They would rather not do anything than risk failure; an alert manager will help them move incrementally toward fulfilling their new roles. They are often surprised that all decisions have to be made without having all the necessary information and that it is much easier to demand input and participation than to be actually responsible for the result of a decision.

Marie Gibbons had been a part of the Carlton Public Library for 12 years. During that time she had often found herself in disagreement with the library managers. However, she was not in a position to make demands for change. She and her colleagues were frustrated but saw little hope for change. The managers were determined to control decision making, answering only to the city council and city manager. Joe, Marie's husband, owned his own small business, and it was unlikely that they would ever move to another location. Marie foresaw many more years of frustration. Each morning as Marie and other staff members drank their coffee in the lounge, they voiced their discontent for the way the library's budget was spent and for how new staff were hired. Marie resigned herself to many more years of cataloging at the public library but began to plan for early retirement.

Then a new city manager was hired. City manager Jeff Powell began to review the policies and procedures in key departments of the city government. The city council, with several new young members recently elected, supported Powell's examination of city departments. A group of parents, interested in increased funding for children's services within the library, voiced their concern for how the library's funds were being expended. Powell earmarked the library as the next department to be reviewed. Library director Frank Small, observing the changes that had taken place in other city departments after Powell had studied their practices, decided to move to a library system in another state.

Marie and her colleagues were hopeful that changes would soon be taking place. Powell, along with the library board, conducted a search for a new director with a managerial style similar to his own. When newly appointed library director Terri Erickson arrived for her first day of work, the staff wasted no time detailing what had been wrong with the former library administration and stating the changes they wanted to see take place.

Powell offered his support to Erickson, encouraging her to make organizational changes. However, after three months with some managers from the former administration still in power, Marie and her colleagues were again beginning to gripe about the library administration.

****

Were staff expectations for immediate changes realistic? Was library director Erickson too cautious? If you were the director, how would you have proceeded? If you were Marie, what would you have done differently?

The staff, unhappy with former library director Small, wanted immediate change when the new director arrived. The changes in other city departments as a result of Powell's review had made them hopeful of quick action when Erickson arrived. They did not realize that Erickson first wanted to assess the present operation of the library and determine what needed to be changed. She also wanted time to determine community expectations of the library and the services that could be offered with the current library budget.

Erickson should have communicated her intent to study the library's problems for a certain time period and use that time to request input from all staff members and the community. Staff should have offered their help in examining the issues and communicated their concern when no action was forthcoming. The city manager should have publicly announced that he wanted the library's problems resolved within a given time period and asked for a proposal, while at the same time expressing his support for Erickson and his confidence that she would handle issues effectively.

ADDRESSING LONG-STANDING PERSONNEL PROBLEMS

Personnel accustomed to an authoritarian administrative style and structure find that hiring managers with a different approach to managing organizations creates unexpected problems. New managers will want to examine the existing organization, identify perceived problems, and define new approaches to problem solving. For staff that primarily wanted a new approach to management and the ability to give input, it may be an uncomfortable realization that with the new style, problems that have lingered beneath the surface for years and to which the organization has maladjusted will come to the forefront and demand to be addressed. The customary, institutionalized methods of problem solving and managing may not be acceptable to a new administrator. Since he or she did not create the problems, a willingness to resolve them will shake the status quo.

Lingering personnel problems, for example, will most likely no longer be brushed aside but will be recognized as potentially harmful to the individuals, the work units, and the organization at large. Longstanding personality conflicts, which are dysfunctional to all involved, will no longer be tolerated but will be addressed. Managers may recommend counseling to employees with personality disorders. Jobs will be redesigned, as tasks, goals, and objectives are examined and changed. Long-established territories may be dismantled and flexibility introduced into scheduling and production. Emphasis will probably change from processes to outcomes. The result will be a departure from calm and stability and a movement toward an evolutionary status.

The catalog department at Normal State College was tolerated by the rest of the library staff. It had long been the department to which malcontented and dysfunctional employees were transferred from other departments. Several members of the catalog department staff had also been hired as a result of pressure from other college departments. Periodically, loud arguments would erupt among staff because it appeared that some member had attempted to sabotage a peer's work. Most employees thought highly of their own work but degraded the quality and quantity of work done by coworkers. There was a lot of finger-pointing and backbiting. A backlog developed and grew. Other departments constantly complained that their work was held up because of the problems in cataloging. The situation was considered impossible, especially since it had existed for many years. Everybody assumed that nothing could be done. Those staff members wishing to transfer to other library departments were unsuccessful because they were viewed as less competent or maladjusted, since they were part of a department that was clearly a problem area.

****

As a new manager, what would you do to change the status quo in the cataloging department?

Libraries often transfer nonproductive or difficult employees to a nonpublic area, where presumably their problems in interacting with colleagues will have a minimal impact on library services. The catalog department, however, is a key department, and problems that develop there have a ripple effect on the organization.

First, the practice of transferring problem employees rather than addressing the problem should be discussed among library managers. Library managers also need to resist pressure from the university to hire individuals without appropriate qualifications. Finally, the staff within the catalog department who engage in inappropriate and disruptive behavior need to be identified, counseled about the problems their behavior causes, and taught to express work-related problems in appropriate ways. If staff members are unwilling or unable to correct their behavior on their own, they may be directed to use an Employee Assistance Program or other counseling services. The library's managers can work with the counseling unit, if appropriate, by providing background information and reinforcing newly acquired positive behaviors.

MANAGING UNCOOPERATIVE EMPLOYEES

Since even under the best circumstances, new managers will find people in their organizations who will not act ethically when faced with changes, who refuse to cooperate, or who decline to contribute to the change effort, managers must be prepared to deal constructively with such a minority while minimizing their influence.

In some instances individuals who do not feel comfortable with the proposed changes will leave voluntarily for more suitable organizations. Sometimes they are old enough that retirement becomes a viable and acceptable option for leaving. Some individuals, however, will experience serious adjustment problems and become stagnant and unproductive. It is management's role to determine why individuals choose to behave inappropriately and undermine organizational change efforts. Direct questions can be asked and instances discussed as they occur. If patterns of resistance persist, despite managerial efforts, problem employees must take part of the responsibility and admit that they no longer fit within the new organization. In such cases, Robert Golembiewski suggests that "the organization should apply its resources to create nonmembers...because it is economically unsound to keep an individual in a job...that has lost allure but which the individual cannot leave without help."[1]

Leigh Jameson had worked for Andrew Duff for several years. However, when problems arose within the interlibrary loan department, Andrew refused to back Leigh when she suggested solutions. As a result, problems cumulated and remained unresolved. When a new assistant director was hired, many of the library staff demanded that Leigh be removed from line responsibilities. Assistant director Mark Gaines talked to different members of the staff, including Leigh, and determined that Leigh had suggested solutions to problems in the past, but when she was repeatedly rebuffed, she had ceased to make suggestions and instead made cynical remarks when a problem was brought to her attention. Andrew insists the problems are a result of Leigh's ineffectual management.

****

What can the new assistant director do about this situation?

First, Gaines should determine what the present unresolved problems are. After making it clear that the problems will now have to be addressed, Gaines can give Andrew and Leigh the opportunity and time to make suggestions for resolution of the problems. Gaines can work with Andrew and Leigh to identify their managerial strengths and give both suggestions on dealing with the problems, if necessary. If Andrew continues to offer excuses rather than working out solutions, Gaines should discuss Andrew's shortcomings with him. If it becomes clear that Andrew lacks managerial skills but has other competencies, he could be given the opportunity to function in a nonmanagerial role within the organization. Gaines may then work with Leigh, and by supporting her suggested solutions and giving her the chance to incorporate change, he can determine if Leigh has managerial potential.

If managerial efforts are successful, positive feedback for well-executed performances will encourage the problem employee to continue his or her adjustment to a new management style. Setbacks and problems are inevitable, but effective managers will help employees understand that progress will not be instantaneous or continuous.

NOTE

1. Robert Golembiewski, "Mid-Life Transitions and Mid-Career Crisis: A Special Case for Individual Development," *Public Administration Review* 38 (March/April 1978): 221.

Chapter 2
Organizational Issues
to Consider

Since the earliest times libraries have been regarded as repositories of forms of information, warehouses for books, periodicals, and media. This perception can be seen in a description of any library; usually, the volume count is supplied early in the verbal or written account of the services. Next, one usually finds the number of serials received by the library on an active basis, then the budget and the number of staff. Any collections of particular value or subject strengths are then detailed.

It has been assumed that such a description will give the reader or potential patron a capsule view of the library's potential value to the user. The purpose of the library as a broker of information is not featured in these descriptions, yet that is exactly what the library is—or is becoming—in the 1980s.

For many years new libraries have accessed databases for their own needs and to meet the information requirements of their clientele. With the development of online catalogs, access to databases is becoming more centralized within each library. This accessibility leads to decentralizing of information dissemination. A patron can now walk up to a terminal or dial into the system from a remote site and query the database of his or her choice.

An increasingly sophisticated clientele no longer relies upon the library to assist in accessing information databases, such as BRS. The user can obtain his or her own password, learn basic search strategies, and access the databases at any time.

Key indexes and reference tools are still being produced in the traditional hard copy, although online access through service bureaus, disks, and in forms using the newly available technology such as CD-ROM is becoming prevalent. As new forms make access easier and more "user friendly" the library finds itself moving from a role as a warehouse of information sources to a role as information broker. This shift affects the library in several ways:

1. The library can explore storage of information through different means rather than continuing to think in terms of larger buildings, remote storage facilities, or more branch libraries.
2. Staff must acquire new skills to assist the patron in developing search strategies using the new media available for the storage of information. The "reference interview" assumes a different importance as staff aid in the accessing of technology and selection of relevant databases.
3. Collection development personnel must concern themselves with compatibility—or incompatibility—of technology and make decisions concerning whether to acquire indexes or other databases in traditional or new formats.
4. Processing staff must determine the best means for providing bibliographic data to the new formats.
5. Acquisition of information in new formats affects the materials allocation, which evolves into an information resources budget. Critical questions affecting the budget must be addressed, such as:

—Will the new information storage media be funded in a traditional manner?

—Will patrons be expected to assume some of the costs of the new information storage?

—Will patrons be expected to defray the costs of online access charges?

—Will traditional hard copy versions of the databases be cancelled with the availability of online access?

These issues must be faced at the same time that libraries are facing shrinking resources. New approaches to and creative analysis of the library budget becomes essential with the acceptance of the library's role as an information broker, an information disseminator using the new technology available.

New criteria for the expenditure of library funds must be developed in order to meet the changing access demands of patrons. As resources shrink and discretionary funds become nonexistent, traditional allocation methodologies will be questioned both by staff and patrons.

A new administrator in a library undergoing change—a library in transition—will find that his or her approach to those two organizational tangibles—personnel and money—can set the tone for success or failure within the transitional organization.

RESOURCE ALLOCATION, MANAGEMENT, AND CONTROL

Libraries, as any organizations, basically have two categories of resources at their disposal: money and people. The future operation of each library or library system is dependent upon how these two resources are effectively allocated, managed, and controlled. The dissemination and utilization of these resources are the bases for power within the organization. Assuming a passive role in regard to these resources will result in an abdication of assigned responsibility. Actively redirecting these resources can help move the organization forward.

The accountability authority for funds and the budgetary process, coupled with the allocation of monies and personnel, carries with it a large measure of power. This power can be misused and abused or fairly managed. The direction is dependent upon the individuals with the accountability authority.

The budgetary process revolves around cost centers, both in the expenditure of monies and the effective and appropriate use of personnel. The allocation of money and personnel is dependent upon an examination of need, which should be based upon the mission of the organization. Unfortunately, the mission of the organization is sometimes overlooked in favor of personal concerns and agendas.

Like other traditional hierarchical organizations, libraries have organized—and often continue to organize—the allocation, management, and control of these resources in strictly and closely controlled ways by involving only the highest administrative level(s) or a small, select group of administrators.

In some libraries, for example, the personnel and operational aspects of the budget are controlled at the senior level while the materials acquisitions budget, now assuming the role of the information resources fund, is monitored and dispensed within the acquisitions area of the library with control being similarly closely held by the acquisitions librarian. Since little or no accountability is required, this may result in situations where some groups end up being favored over others as funds are dispersed.

The privilege to allocate and control resources, when granted to a select group, too often—deserved or not—fostered suspicions, unfairness, and abuses. With strict control, there is limited access to information about the availability of resources. Narrowly defined control is usually regarded by the individuals outside the select group as a methodology by which power can be contained within a small group or even with one individual. Of course, not all containing of control within a narrowly defined group is bad.

A new administrator in any organization is wise to review the existing methodology used for authority or control of funds and to ascertain how the total budget is allocated among personnel, operational needs, and materials acquisition. Responsibility issues should be closely examined. An analysis of several years of budget activity is most appropriate and useful. A new manager in a transitional organization should be alert to comments about budgetary control issues. The disenfranchised staff, those who were allowed only limited knowledge and control of funds, will be vocal. Their comments may be valid or they may reflect jealousy. Comments from clientele will reflect their perception of favoritism.

From almost the first day on, Catherine Remington, the new library director, heard complaints about how the materials budget had been allocated and how little funding had been set aside for the sciences. When she queried Louise Bergman, the acquisitions librarian, about these complaints, Louise insisted that the funds had been expended in a manner that fulfilled the demands of patrons. There had been little demand for materials voiced by the science group within the university. Gretchen Roe, however, who had been on the staff for many years, insisted that the scientists had simply become frustrated with the lack of responsiveness on the part of Louise and had ceased complaining, instead resorting to the creation of reading rooms with core collections to meet their needs.

Catherine also heard complaints from staff that the technical services portion of the library was overstaffed while the public services staff struggled to staff service points during peak use hours. When she queried Steve Kendrick, who was in charge of technical services, he justified the staffing configuration with arguments about lack of processing backlogs, the size of the acquisitions budget, and the complexity of the tasks assigned to the technical services staff.

Another issue brought to Catherine's attention was the large number of students assigned to circulation. Negative comments were made by staff observing student assistants studying and socializing in that department, while students in other areas were constantly busy and hard-working.

As Catherine listened to staff comments, she observed defensiveness on the part of Steve and Louise and bitterness and suspicions on the part of other staff members. She grew increasingly concerned about the disparity of opinions she encountered concerning the acquisitions and personnel budgets.

Catherine realized that she had two avenues to pursue. She could accept the present situation and assume, as Steve and Louise insisted, that the staff not involved in the budget process lacked a basic knowledge of the needs of the library and that their jealousies and suspicions were inevitable. Or, she could conduct her own investigation, analyze the situation, and if necessary, involve other employees in restructuring the budget to meet current needs of all subject areas.

After studying the expenditure pattern for acquisitions, Catherine discovered that over a period of several years by far the majority of the money had been dispersed to the humanities and the social sciences even though the materials in those areas were less expensive than those in the sciences. She also discovered that numerous reading rooms existed in the buildings housing the science departments; as a result, substantial amounts of university resources were being spent for materials housed outside the library.

As she examined work flow in the technical services area, she learned that policies created decades before and no longer relevant were still being enforced, needlessly complex procedures were in place, and tasks were duplicated by different units within technical services.

In circulation, students were indeed on the job in disproportionate numbers during slow activity periods even though there was a requirement for books to be reshelved within two hours.

****

By analyzing the situation and reprioritizing needs, Catherine can readjust resources to better serve the library's clientele. Simultaneously she can also undertake a reeducation program for those individuals who controlled the resources that have been reallocated or she can assign the authority to individuals who do not use the control of resources as a power ploy.

Even if a new manager does not find such suspicions and perceptions, narrowly defined scopes of resource control mean that only limited experience in managing resources will exist within the organization. If the control group disbands or the administrator in the authority position leaves the organization, the knowledge of the bureaucratic system, the organizational structure of the resources allocation, and the managerial expertise also disappear. The resulting situation is an organization that must reestablish that experience level and perhaps completely redesign the allocation, management, and control mechanisms under crisis conditions.

When this happens it should be understood and expected that for a time the organization will experience difficulties and frustrations as the few remaining individuals with a knowledge base of the resources allocation policies and procedures attempt to explain to the new managers how the organization has functioned in the past. The new managers will then need to define their own approach to resource allocation, management, and control as they also work toward an understanding of the institutional process. Also, individuals formerly not involved in the budgeting process or formerly not privy to information about resource allocation and management must be taught the process. These people may very well have problems understanding the process and will at first make inappropriate decisions based on their lack of knowledge and comprehension.

Managers in institutions in transition, especially those institutions moving from a strict hierarchical structure to one emphasizing participative management and team leadership, will find themselves confronted with individuals who are eager to be involved in the decision-making process in allocating resources, a process from which they had been formerly excluded. These same individuals will have limited experience in managing and controlling the allocated resources and a training period will be necessary. The allocation process can be used to educate people not only about the budgetary process but also about organizational goals, priorities, resource opportunities, and the organizational constraints; this education process should decrease suspicions about the overall administration.

In order to involve different levels of staff in the resources decision-making, managers themselves, in addition to staff, must be willing to go through an education process. Management must be ready to delegate part of the decision-making authority and spell out the necessary limitations.

With delegation must go respect for the decision making. Management must understand that constant checking and exerting of control or even the appearance of exerting control is not appropriate once delegation has taken place and is being effectively handled. It also is not conducive to establishing a trust relationship. Staff to whom this authority has been delegated and to whom this new responsibility now goes must understand their new accountability responsibility. It is very easy for staff to insist on input into resource allocation, management, and control without realizing the decision making, the responsibility, and the effort that goes into the tasks.

Responsiveness is necessary on the part of administrators delegating utilization and control of resources as well as on the part of staff receiving these new responsibilities. Education of staff in the library and institutional policies and procedures that must be adhered to must come before responsibilities can be effectively delegated and managed. Managers must also be aware of the need for them to let staff take risks and make mistakes as they assume new responsibilities.

As new managers work with staff in learning the institutional processes and in delegating authority, they should also be aware that there may be great resistance from those individuals still within the organization who formerly held complete control or authority and who now find their power or authority being dispersed. An example of such a situation might be an acquisitions librarian, such as Louise in our example, who has had total control over the purchasing decisions and the dispersal of monies and who now finds that the purchasing and resource allocation decisions are being distributed throughout a group of subject bibliographers. Such an individual may feel very threatened and may try to sabotage the dispersal of this authority.

As cost centers are reviewed, structure analyzed, and needs reexamined, other issues to be addressed surface, waiting to be addressed as the overall change effort progresses.

SPACE UTILIZATION AND ERGONOMICS

Libraries built during the earlier part of this century usually had a single large reference room that was crowded with long study tables with study lamps to compensate for the high ceiling and ineffectual lighting from the ceiling fixtures and from the tall windows. These reference rooms were often the only area of the library where patrons could go, since the stacks were closed and the processing areas were off limits. The stacks, in contrast to the reference room, were characterized by low ceilings, narrow aisles, and lighting fixtures that were turned on at the end of individual stack aisles. The processing section of the library was crowded with desks, manual typewriters, and stacks of catalog cards, request slips, and duplicate reference bibliographies for verifying bibliographic information. Few offices were provided for staff. In general the libraries were rather dark and gloomy places.

As libraries moved toward open stacks, building planners—librarians, architects, and interior designers—changed to modular designs with bays designated by columns, nonload-bearing walls that could theoretically be easily dismantled, lower ceilings in public service and processing areas with better lighting, and numerous electrical outlets to accommodate the increased use of technology. These new library buildings were lighter and airy and much more pleasant places in which to work and study.

Today both types of libraries are often caught by surprise and find that their buildings are too old to easily accommodate the new technology. Rewiring and reconfiguration of work and patron space are often necessary or else the buildings have to be completely remodeled. Even fairly recently constructed buildings often lack adequate wiring and sufficient lighting and outlets.

Since libraries are usually housed in buildings constructed when needs and philosophies were different from today, managers of transitional organizations may find that space utilization becomes a top priority to be reviewed in light of the library's new role as an information broker. The introduction of new technologies, such as online catalogs, requires creative use of existing space and demands better planning for the future use of available space. At a minimum, managers will see the addition of electrical power poles in order to place outlets where they are needed, conduits placed along existing walls and columns, raised flooring to provide space for adequate wiring of electrical and data lines, and utilization of work stations rather than standard desks and offices.

Office landscaping is incorporated into staff work areas to provide flexible, nonpermanent yet private work areas for staff. Microcomputers and terminals dedicated to online use demand acquisitions of workstations that will fill the needs of many users. If used by multiple operators, the workstations should have shelving for manuals; space for the terminal or micro; adjacent space for a printer; work space for data sheets or the materials being processed; or space for a book truck. Lighting should be shielded to reduce glare or the terminals should have (or be modified for) nonglare screens. If noise from printers or group work in an area is a problem, acoustic partitions should be used.

When workstations are for single users, they may incorporate most features as an office, providing desk work space, files, space for the microcomputer and its peripherals, online capability, as well as proper lighting and acoustic considerations.

New technologies demand that we now be concerned not only with lighting appropriate to the work being performed but also the amount of time individuals are allowed to work on CRTs, the effects of glare and ionization on the worker, stress levels as a result of routine inputting, heights of work stations, and seating appropriate to the work being performed.

For most of us these are relatively new developments. We may have already resolved the issue of length of work periods online, something we didn't usually worry much about in the days of the typewriter; however, we may still be forcing these new work tools into the old desk, table, and chair configurations that have survived from the manual work days. Now suddenly we must be concerned with work stations being the best level for the average staff member, monitors that can be tilted or moved to accommodate different visual needs, printers that are low in noise level, and chairs that have five-point, stable pedestals, broader seats, and adjustability in height and tilt of the back piece.

All of these considerations fall under the heading of a relatively new term: ergonomics. For managers this means no longer plopping terminals onto any available table or expecting staff to use any chair that swivels. For most organizations, this emphasis on ergonomics has meant major investments in new equipment and furniture. For libraries where traditionally the "pretty" furniture was placed in the patron areas, with castoffs used in "staff only" work areas, this has meant a major reversal of attitudes and philosophies. Staff using the wonders of technological advancement now also need work stations and equipment that accommodate their physical needs rather than "making do."

Ergonomics and work periods on terminals have become issues—often union issues—to be negotiated between groups of workers and management. Debates are ongoing on the effect of long periods of terminal work—or working on terminals at all—by pregnant women. Providing eye exams for terminal workers has become another issue of debate.

As Melissa Moore, the new library director, examined the use of resources, she found that her predecessor had exerted total control over the operational budget, limited the purchase of needed supplies and appropriate furniture and equipment, dispersing the latter only to favored staff. The result was an ergonomically poor work facility with staff struggling to accomplish tasks without adequate resources.

Melissa also discovered that a few favored staff members had an inordinate amount of power within the organization to the resentment of the rest of the staff.

David Grant, Melissa's predecessor, had used his authority to exert control over the work flow and the allocation of resources in the public library. This placed him in a position of total control of the organization with little delegation of responsibility to individuals on the staff except those he chose to favor with additional resources. When David left the organization, staff resentments became more evident. One of Melissa's priorities became the review of the dispersal of operational monies, and the acquisition of appropriate resources for the work place was necessary.

The bottom line for managers in libraries is that we can no longer expect staff to tolerate marginal or outdated workplaces. Even if a major renovation of work areas and replacement of all equipment is not possible, some incorporation of good ergonomic ideas is essential. This may be accomplished by the acquisition of comfortable and appropriate seating, purchase of workstations of the proper height for terminals, placing of terminals to minimize glare, addition of utility poles where outlets are needed, replacement of desks as finances allow, regrouping of work areas to accommodate the new technology and the utilization of different tools to accomplish new tasks. Rather than purchasing new electrical typewriters, libraries can acquire electronic typewriters with memory and microcomputers, which can be used with application software or as terminals to minis and main frames and offsite systems.

If new facilities are being designed or a major renovation is underway, experts can be consulted to help design the best work areas ergonomically. However, relatively few new libraries are being planned and designed today, and with resources limited for the foreseeable future, it may be out of the question to hire facility design consultants. Monies for renovation or equipment replacement are likely to remain limited.

There are other approaches that management can take, however. In a community, interior designers may be willing to donate some of their time to assist library staff in improving their work areas. On campuses, interior or architectural design classes may undertake an analysis and redesign of work areas as a class project. Both approaches will have mixed results but will at least be a start for discussion and generate different ideas.

At the very least, staff willing to address ergonomic problems in the workplace can be enlisted in task forces or problem-specific committees and charged with problem identification and suggestions for the acquisition of ergonomically correct equipment. Such groups can research height, lighting, space, and hardware requirements. Then, based on funding available, the groups can prioritize needs so that work space can be improved within a specific timetable. For example, acquisition of proper work stations and seating for terminals used by multiusers all day should be a first priority. Acquisition of workstations and seating for microcomputers used frequently but not full time could be the next priority. Replacement of unsatisfactory private consultation space for managers might be another priority. Carpeting and acoustic barriers and replacement of improper lighting might take a lower priority position if the major problems are workstations and seating. Unfortunately, in too many libraries the provision of sufficient electrical outlets or properly placed data lines may be a larger problem than the workstations and other equipment presently provided. Suffice it to say that site preparation has not kept pace with the advancement and incorporation of new technology into the workplace. Inappropriate space utilization can become an organizational issue and should be acknowledged, analyzed, and accommodated before it becomes a major point of discussion and debate.

ORGANIZATIONAL STRUCTURES

As libraries are changing from highly structured institutions to environments in which people cooperate with each other, they jointly search for the solutions to their problems. These organizational changes are gaining momentum because:

1. the larger environment places new and different demands and constraints on libraries
2. the missions and goals of libraries have broadened considerably
3. new technologies have imposed new data and behavior requirements
4. people with different educational and cultural backgrounds, expectations, and attitudes are entering library employment.

Traditional library management was based on rationality in decision making and quantitative analysis. The subtle and subjective components of management were largely ignored in favor of the semblance of objectivity, logic, and order. Much of the decision making was centralized at the senior level.

Today library managers are trying to foster broader participation in decision making. The relationships between managers and workers are becoming more reciprocal, reflecting the influence of democratic American values. Workers are expecting and demanding more involvement and influence in the decision-making processes. Managers are no longer able or willing to control all aspects of the decision-making and planning processes. They want to share the responsibility as well as the credit or blame for the results. More managers also understand that they are responsible for training the managers of the future and that one way to create the next generation of managers is to involve staff at all levels in the planning and decision-making processes.

Before undertaking a concerted effort to change a library's organizational structure, managers should determine their own biases and subjective views on organizational arrangements. While it is fashionable and almost mandatory to espouse participative management or team management, it is quite a different matter to implement organizational changes that will lead to increased staff involvement in decision making.

Library organization is traditionally based on McGregor's Theory X philosophy, which prescribes that:

1. Organizations should be differentiated into specialized functional tasks.
2. Subordinates should pursue individual tasks with concern only for the completion of their narrowly defined tasks.
3. There will be rigid chains of commands.
4. There will be detailed and exhaustive job descriptions.
5. The overall picture of the organization is only relevant to those at the top of the hierarchy.
6. Communication follows vertical lines along the chain of command.
7. Behavior is governed by superiors.
8. Emphasis is on narrow, specialized knowledge rather than general, complete knowledge.

Most organizational changes in the first half of this century tried to establish and apply the above principles in American organizations. They were based on time and motion studies, job analysis, job descriptions, design of mechanistic control systems, and revisions of organizational charts. In most cases the changes were worked out by technocrats, then legislated from the top and implemented through the hierarchy. Assumptions were that technical considerations are the most important and will in turn lead to greater effectiveness and efficiency.

Hierarchical organizations generate a climate of efficiency, briskness, and apparent high level of activity. Individuals at the top can view the organization in its entirety and place details into a larger, broader context. Employees are encouraged to work hard and accomplish their assigned tasks without much questioning—or without much explanation forthcoming.

Studies have shown that about 50 percent of the population feels very comfortable in hierarchical organizations. The expectation is that people will behave in a logical manner with the focus on getting things done. The general population assumes that the world of work is shaped like a pyramid, with a few on top and many on the bottom. They respect authority, rely on logic and proven procedures, and believe that if all schedules, procedures, and timetables were clearly enforced, the world would be an efficient, comfortable place that would in turn also sustain the day-to-day operations of any organization.

Many librarians who have chosen the profession because it appeared safe, comfortable, orderly, and respectable fall into this category of employee that is most comfortable with this hierarchical structure. They respond to change by contracting rather than expanding their options. They are fearful of losing their place of importance within an organization and fail to recognize that change can increase their opportunities for personal and professional growth and managerial innovation.

Such employees react to change as leading only to turbulent, uncertain times. They feel most comfortable when they are given specific new procedures and modes of operation. If their capacities are not stretched to the limits, they will again settle down and become the stabilizing and perhaps stagnant components of an organization.

Managers charged with implementing change should expect that during the actual change process, these employees will focus on single issues critical to them as individuals and within their perception of personal power. They may start to emphasize their control over others and begin to rigidly enforce rules, regulations, and procedures.

Carol Leeds had worked within the library for several years and had achieved a supervisory position. She relished her position of power and enjoyed the deferential treatment she received from subordinates. She had very definite ideas about the role of a manager and the power that rested in such a position. She had the ear of library director Joe Lawrence and he consulted her on most issues.

When a new director was hired, he began to talk to individual members of the staff and seek ideas for policy and procedural changes that might be considered. Carol, wishing to make an impression on the new director as a good manager, began to question her own staff about their ideas for change. Several staff were reluctant to share the same ideas they had expressed to the new director with Carol. Carol began to enforce work schedules, insisted on strict adherence to procedures, and talked to the new director about her own effective management style and philosophies of management.

****

Carol was feeling threatened when the managerial style of the administration changed and the new director evidenced interest in staff ideas. When staff realized that they could openly express their ideas to the chief librarian, they began to resist Carol's attempt at control. She in turn tried to learn what suggestions they were making to the new director, fearful that the suggestions might include some with which she was uncomfortable. In an attempt to control the flow of ideas, Carol exerted control over the work lives of the workers. She felt that in her own position rested power over the lives and ideas of staff.

What could be done to bring about change during this period?

To help their employees grow and adapt during such stressful times, managers may assign them to work in settings that are contrary to their personality styles. Employees who are comfortable only in structured environments may be asked to work in quality circles, committees, and task forces where they can learn to share their concerns and problems and have to take other points of view under serious consideration. Employees who refuse to change will inevitably fall behind and will lose the control and power they held in the former atmosphere.

Requirements for managers and leaders become more complex in times of change. To lead and manage during such times requires vision, imagination, sensitivity, and the ability to alleviate stress in others. They must understand that people will react differently to the managerial style changes.

If, however, managers within an organization that is undergoing change formed their own expectations in hierarchical organizations and feel comfortable with those expectations, they will want to keep a tight rein instead of adjusting to ambiguity. They will fail to explain the need for change adequately to their subordinates and will relate their actions as carrying out the wishes or instructions of their own superiors. To minimize their own discomfort with change, they will expect subordinates to implement directives without question. If there are questions, they will explain the directive as being what the director insists upon.

Managers comfortable with the old structured environment will devote little planning to the new change effort because they are unable and unwilling to envision and seriously consider the contingency of change. If, however, these managers accept that change is inevitable and allow themselves to grow with the changes, they will, with time, recognize the benefits of other organizational structures for the different tasks to be performed.

While they may still be most comfortable in emphasizing the necessity for operational rules and procedures, they will also start to recognize the value of social interactions and the need to take individual differences into consideration. The more open they become, the more they will recognize that employees' growth and life cycles are not necessarily the same as the organization's and that some friction, conflict, and problems are normal. As their understanding of self and others grows, such managers will take more risks, delegate more responsibilities, and become less involved in the immediate tasks.

PARALLEL ORGANIZATIONS

Since existing organizational structures are often too rigid to respond to the rapid changes experienced in today's work environment, models of new organizational arrangements are emerging, providing alternatives by creating "parallel organizations" that can be integrated into existing bureaucracies. Stein and Moss Kanter characterize parallel structures as flat and flexible, but also as formal, problem-solving and governance organizations that serve to supplement bureaucracies and exist side by side with them, not to replace them.

Bureaucratic structures are most effective for maintaining production and the routinization of useful procedures. They are used to define job titles, pay grades, fixed reporting relationships, and formal tasks and cannot be completely replaced. The challenge of administrators is to decide which tasks can be best performed by bureaucratic structures while creating what Howard Carlson at General Motors calls the parallel organization.

The latter is not to be confused with the informal organization; rather it is a formal structure that seeks to institutionalize responsiveness, participation, and problem solving. If properly designed, it will provide opportunities and power bases in addition to those inherent in bureaucracies, increasing the quality of work life of people who are usually without formal power and resources. Parallel organizations provide opportunities to develop and grow, making organizations more responsive to environmental pressures. The result is better communication, problem-solving and planning skills, better interpersonal relations, improved motivation and morale, higher productivity, increased supervisory skills, and better use of resources. Through the use of parallel organizations, employees are grouped in new ways, giving them challenging opportunities to learn and grow, accessing resources and power.

The concurrent use of bureaucratic and parallel organizations involves employees in two ways through different, but formal, structures. It expands the job opportunities of participants by means other than promotion and institutionalizes creativity.

In summary, the past hierarchical structures were very similar from library to library, with the number of senior administrators and mix of departments reporting to them being the primary variations. The 1980s are seeing more experimentation with organizational hierarchies of libraries.

These variations in structure are mainly brought about by financial constraints, technology, available personnel, and new philosophies about management and the library profession. It can be expected that experimentation with structural variations will continue for some time. Not all staff will be comfortable with the evolving structures. Insecurities will become more evident in some individuals, while others will thrive on the situation. Managers should be aware of the changes taking place in other libraries, be receptive to incorporating new organizational structures into their own libraries as appropriate, and be cognizant of the reaction of staff to such changes.

COMMUNICATION PATTERNS IN HIERARCHIES

Communication in hierarchical organizations is used to:

- get results
- accomplish organizational tasks
- clarify lines of authority
- give direction and guidance to others

It emphasizes formal channels, where people on the lower rungs of the organizational ladder are often inhibited from communicating upward for fear of negative consequences. Directional communication is primarily downward, although informational communication will also exist at the peer level.

Clarence Griffin had worked for an authoritarian manager in a public library, and he adopted a similar management style. Clarence's areas of responsibility included the condition of the library's physical facilities. He preferred to work with the city's facilities staff himself and he did not share any knowledge of the maintenance operation with other staff.

One day when library staff arrived at work, they observed plumes of steam coming from the building. As they entered the library, the atmosphere was humid, musty, and generally unpleasant. Judy Campbell, a library clerk, saw Clarence and asked him what the problem was. Clarence replied, "This happens periodically. Don't be concerned."

****

Do you believe Clarence's response was appropriate?

Clarence preferred to control information concerning his area of responsibility. To keep staff ignorant, he communicated only what was absolutely necessary. Considering the authoritarian managerial style with which Clarence was accustomed, this approach was not unexpected. What would have been a better response to staff questions?

Senior managers in hierarchical organizations expect their subordinates to communicate mainly to:

- confirm the status
- identify problems related to work
- analyze the importance of such problems before communicating them
- bring alternatives to the attention of others in order to solve the problems

These hierarchical senior managers in turn expect to communicate with their employees to:

• confirm the value of the individual to the organization
• explain decisions
• present explanations and sufficient information on particular issues under consideration
• clarify their expectations of an employee's performance

Informal and Formal Organizational Networks

There is another organizational structure with which we must deal—the informal organization network. Within all organizations, the informal channels address issues and problems and attempt to resolve them outside the hierarchical structure. The results are uneven at best. The informal network resolves issues based on the needs and talents of the individuals involved. Political issues are at stake. Informal power that rests with the individuals involved becomes a critical element in the resolution of problems. Old rivalries surface and the tension mounts as stresses increase.

As a result, within the traditional organizational structure, resolution of problems and the creation of informal policies and procedures become inconsistent, while matters appear to proceed at an even pace until one of these inconsistencies becomes an issue and a new problem arises. At that point, the rigid hierarchy exerts control and the informal network finds itself reprimanded by the official organizational hierarchy. The result may be a harsh mandate or a resolution to the matter that is inconsistent with the issue under consideration.

Under the traditional organizational structures within which most of us have spent our careers, there has been and will continue to be a rigid hierarchy through which we functioned—or in spite of which we functioned. The existing structure may have been very unbending, with strict adherence to following line communication channels as dictated by the organizational structure. Thus, no decisions or serious examination of issues was allowed unless the senior administrators were involved in the discussion or those administrators had granted permission for middle management to communicate directly.

Middle management in turn might or might not allow the individuals directly involved in the situation to communicate directly. Much time would be expended in adhering to the organizational protocol as it was interpreted within the formal hierarchy.

In addition if communication between divisions or units is primarily at the senior or middle management levels, the staff primarily concerned with discussing the issue or critical to the resolution of the problem may never be involved and the salient points never expressed. Thus, the issues or the problem may not be adequately addressed or resolved. Or the surface concerns may be addressed but the depth of the issues or problems will be ignored.

Previously, this might have been an adequate situation when time and money were not such critical factors. Now time and money and the concerns of staff are all major issues that can no longer be overlooked or dealt with peripherally. There is little flexibility or margin for error; we no longer have the luxury of resolving problems only through a rigid, established hierarchy.

Informal organizational networks thrive, especially within traditional management environments, and new managers who discount their importance will experience many unexpected frustrations.

This informal organizational structure is one on which the functioning of the organization is very dependent; it is indeed the force which controls the ongoing operations of the library.

Such informal networks or communication channels thrive within libraries. Managers may think they direct the day-to-day operation of the library but in reality this informal network is in control of the library. While this may be of concern to some managers, benevolent managers who practice a laissez-faire approach to control of the organization won't consider this an issue.

A rigid, control-conscious manager may feel threatened by the informal network and start making a concerted effort to obliterate it. However, even if the network must go underground, it will still exist and flourish. In fact, if a strong attempt is made to destroy it, the network will probably increase in power and become stronger than ever, with more staff becoming a part of it, with often disastrous results for the manager.

Within libraries in transition and undergoing changes, with new managers asserting themselves and the structure of the organization evolving, this informal network can afford to be observant and analytical of events that transpire, biding its time. The informal network will be ready to assist with the transition—or be prepared to hinder it.

The informal network may elect to observe the situation for a lengthy period before entering the fray. It will detect the strengths and weaknesses of the new managers, determine the direction the evolving organization is moving in, and eventually make a decision whether to support or hinder it.

The informal network will evaluate sections of the transitional organization and may choose to have portions of the evolving organization survive and thrive while letting others disintegrate or even actively participating in their collapse. Survival and disintegration may be dependent upon several factors:

- the management technique used
- the communication mode incorporated
- the personnel employed to initiate change
- personalities
- outside events

The network may refuse to accept some of the changes either because the network members disapprove of the changes or because the change implementors are not accepted or respected. If the situation is allowed to continue and is not addressed, the library may very well continue to function, but there will exist two levels within the organization: the visible one that is in charge officially and the invisible one that in reality now controls the organization and undermines or supports as it sees fit. Once again political issues and power bases will become an issue and the organization will find itself hindered from future progress.

When Charley Hogan arrived at Lykes Public Library, he discovered that an informal network had run the library for several years under a weak administration. Charley wanted to be in control so when his counterpart in public services was hired, Charley persuaded him to assist in influencing the director to issue a strong memo, reiterating the line authority they both had. Tom Simpson, in public services, was uncomfortable with the memo but it seemed important to Charley so he went along with it.

Tom analyzed the strengths and weaknesses of the staff and took time to learn the organizational history. He began to use the talents of the stronger members of the staff who had also been part of the informal network that had kept the library functioning effectively. Tom had a relaxed administrative style and gained the confidence of the staff reporting to him.

In the meantime, Charley insisted on approving and disapproving every action in his division and instructed his staff to carefully observe line authority. He always insisted that Tom and he communicate directly on all matters.

****

What is the likely result of Charley's management style at the Lykes Public Library?

Tom and Charley will inevitably be compared. Staff reporting to Charley will become resentful of the relaxed atmosphere in Tom's area. Morale will suffer. In the end, Tom will probably have more personal power within the organization and Charley may find himself in an ineffectual position within the organization.

In a library undergoing change and attempting to survive in a transitional phase, it is important for the administration to understand that inevitably an informal network exists and is waiting in the wings, undecided whether or not to participate or allow the new management to survive and thrive.

The network may initially decide to be supportive, but this support can easily erode if new players are introduced or the weaknesses of managers begin to surface. When the latter happens, the network will once again step back and assess the situation and may adopt a different approach to management of the transitional organization.

Rather than attempting to change an organization without involving the network, management should adopt an approach similar to that of the network: observe and analyze the situation. The leaders of the informal organization will soon become obvious. If they can be identified and their strengths and weaknesses determined, these leaders can be used and incorporated into the change process, and they can become in fact the implementors and cheerleaders for change.

Care should be taken in determining the leaders. A flawed identification will result in increased problems. The political power structure within the informal organization should be carefully observed since setting opposing, powerful leaders on collision paths will result in chaos and will hinder change. Selecting people outside the informal network and granting them excessive power or responsibility will similarly hinder change. Assigning authority to individuals who do not have the support of the staff will severely hamper desired progress and will result in fragmentation within the organization. Compartmentalization of effort will take place and the informal network will assess the situation and determine where it wishes to throw its support. The segments not receiving the favor of the informal organization will in turn find themselves at a disadvantage in achieving their desired goals, even if the senior administration is behind the out-of-favor segments. The informal structure within the organization will again stand back and observe and analyze until it is ready to take a position.

In transitional organizations, administrators should enlist the assistance of the informal organization and direct the energies of that network in implementing change. With the support and enthusiasm of the informal structure and the appropriate use of the leaders in implementing change, the formal organization will find itself making changes expeditiously and with less stress and chaos.

Using the power of the leaders will decrease opposition, although there may also be turnover in personnel during this process as the network leaders engage in their own power struggle. On the periphery will be the nonplayers who are observing the changes and watching the power struggle both on the official and unofficial levels. These nonplayers will continue to function within their positions and will engage in the changes only if they support the key participants in the change process.

Members of the informal organization can also be incorporated into the hierarchy by giving them formal position power and using their particular talents and power within the organization. This is in fact an excellent long-term strategy, ensuring that informal leaders share also the responsibilities that are inherent in exercising power.

The administration that effectively uses the informal organization in incorporating changes should also recognize the likelihood of old rivalries surfacing; these should not be ignored but rather should be examined and addressed so that the organization is not left in turmoil.

If the administration chooses to implement change through reliance and utilization of the informal organizational structure, it should first spend some time in not only identifying the leaders within the informal structure but in also learning the history of the library organization. Every library has an oral history, some of which is based on gossip, much of which is based on bias, underlying all of which is the factual history that explains how the library organization reached its current state. Administrators who tap into this oral history will find themselves better able to use and direct the informal organization and its leaders. Learning how rivalries developed, how power has been achieved by certain leaders, and what caused biases to enter the picture all will help the administrators understand their own roles and the roles to be played by the informal leaders.

It is not unusual in any organization, including libraries, for some authority to be achieved by individuals through means that the informal organization does not support. This positional authority does not necessarily mean organizational power, especially if the invisible network is not supportive. A new administrative structure can identify those individuals who achieved positional authority through means not supported by the informal structure by being observant of the behavior of members of the invisible network, especially the behavior of the leaders of that network.

Patrick Nordstrom enjoyed his authority as director of a major university library in the eastern part of the state. The authority he had at work helped him overlook his unhappy marriage. He enjoyed the "perks" of being the director. When he went to conferences, the recognition he received as director of an important university library led him to make the acquaintance of many librarians from other libraries.

When Patrick was asked to speak at a nearby state conference, he took advantage of the opportunity to spend some time away from his wife and family. It was there that he met Glenda Hunter. Glenda was in awe of Patrick's title and repeatedly told him how much she had heard about him and respected him. When a vacancy occurred at Patrick's library, Glenda applied for the position. Patrick knew her so he hired her without consulting other staff.

When Glenda arrived, the other staff soon noticed her special relationship with the director. Glenda spent as much time with Patrick as she could, always alerting him of her achievements on assignments. When merit raises were awarded, Patrick, pleased with Glenda's efforts, usually gave her a substantial salary adjustment.

Then, Patrick was in an automobile accident and was forced into disability retirement. The new director was approached by Glenda, who wasted no time in relaying her past accomplishments and new achievements to him. The new director was impressed with the progress Glenda had made and investigated how she had made such strides so he could guide other staff in a similar manner. The new director soon learned that Glenda's accomplishments could not always be substantiated, and he began to question any new achievements she related to him. When raises were next awarded, Glenda, for the first time, received none.

****

Glenda had promoted herself based on her friendship with Patrick, who did not examine how effective she was within the organization. Since Glenda's role within the library was dependent upon Patrick being the director, when he was no longer in a position of authority, it was necessary for Glenda to prove herself to the new administrator. The new administrator found that Glenda was not as effective a librarian as she stated and Glenda soon ceased to be a key player within the organization.

While a new administration should not necessarily censure the targets of the invisible network, it should be wary of appearing irrationally supportive of those individuals until the administration has determined the reasons and extent of the antagonism. Assigning increased authority or responsibility to these staff members early, or refusing to acknowledge even privately that there is friction, will hinder the administration's attempts to bring about major change, which needs to be supported by the informal organization.

The potential problems with staff toward whom the invisible network directs its antagonism can be at least partially offset by not paying undue attention to these individuals and limiting their access to increased authority and responsibility, while the reasons for the antagonism are studied. It may even be necessary to encourage or insist on these individuals leaving the organization altogether if the degree of animosity to overcome is too great. Ignoring the existence of the problem will not lead to the disappearance of the problem but only its exacerbation. This in turn may lead to dysfunction within all or part of the organization and a loss of confidence in the new administration and its goals. The informal network will also engage in its own censuring of the administration and the individuals who are its targets.

In summary, a new administration directing a library through changes and transitions can implement change with more momentum if it will quickly learn the oral history of the existing organization, determine the informal structure that is presently within the library, identify its leaders and their strengths and weaknesses, enlist the support of this informal network, determine the targets of its animosities, and determine why they are targets. There may be justifiable reasons why they became the focus of the informal network.

Chapter 3
Creation of a New
Organizational Environment

Once the manager of a library in transition has thoroughly analyzed the history and the major players of an organization, he or she can work out strategic plans to move toward more organic organizational structures.

Certainly one of the most important tasks of top management implementing organizational change is to make critical decisions concerning the creation of a more democratic and tolerant organizational culture. Questions arise about which values need to be shared; what objectives have priority; what belief systems the employees should share; and how past and current events should be interpreted.

Besides top management, work groups have a very high influence on the creation of organizational cultures. In highly structured organizations, work groups tend to focus on accomplishments and reward those individuals who achieve their work goals. They may also establish destructive norms by exercising excessive control and inhibiting freedom of expression.

For organizations and individuals to change, the norms established by the work groups often need to change. Managers not aware of the group dynamics in changing organizations may excessively reward those individuals who are willing to support new organizational goals and thereby create disapproval for them by the nonsupportive work group. For new behaviors to take root and succeed, group norms themselves will need to change simultaneously; otherwise new organizational procedures and policies will not be implemented.

To bring about organizational change from a hierarchical structure to a more participative environment, the underlying assumptions of the organization must be openly analyzed. Patterns of behavior that have remained unquestioned and have become acceptable are not easily challenged.

To change organizational group norms, managers need to take a fresh look at what is happening in their organizations. Individuals often do not see what is actually happening around them; rather, they see what they want to see, what they are comfortable with, and what is most familiar.

If they are asked to actually observe and record behavior for a set time period, their observation skills will increase, and their awareness of group actions and directions will heighten. Observations of how people are actually communicating with each other will add further information about group interactions. Managers should ask themselves questions like: How do people make contacts with each other? How do they speak to each other? Are they open, restrained, aggressive, warm, or angry?

While we cannot always see why people interact in certain ways, we can make assumptions about the reasons for types of interaction and discuss these assumptions with other managers. This enables us to check our perceptions for degrees of reality before drawing conclusions about communication patterns.

Libraries today are faced with many organizational decisions. They can refuse to change because their decision makers do not see detrimental consequences to continuing with their current organizational structure. Problems created may slowly increase, but as long as opportunities for action are overlooked, the chances for serious organizational or managerial failure will escalate.

Many library managers will acknowledge a need for change, but they may choose incremental adjustments rather than major strategic change, leaving the organization maladjusted and unable to cope with increasing demands and expectations for change. Library managers can also avoid dealing with critical organizational issues. Many will give up hope for solutions, even though they perceive the serious risks for the organizational future. Others will continue to search for the perfect solution, delaying action until a crisis erupts.

The most productive approach is a state of constant vigilance, wherein managers perceive serious risks and search for solutions in a timely manner.

ESTABLISHING OR REESTABLISHING CREDIBILITY WITHIN THE LIBRARY

Establishing or reestablishing credibility is critical to the success of new administrators. They must quickly gain credibility and support from an often wary staff, which is suspicious of what the new administration will want to do. Administrators already in place who have lost credibility will find it a difficult task to reestablish it. Once trust is lost, it is virtually impossible to regain. A case study illustrates.

Assistant Director of Technical Services Don Burton is in the position of having to replace his head of acquisitions, Carl Dennison, who had taken a job out of state. Carl had been well-liked and had done a good job, often standing up to Don when he felt Don was making an inappropriate decision. The staff regretted Carl's departure but congratulated him on being offered a better job elsewhere.

The new fiscal year was just beginning and it was critical that ordering of requested items take place as quickly as possible. A librarian on the staff, Bobby Crowe, appeared to be eager to assume the acquisitions responsibility so Don appointed him on an interim basis. Bobby had never worked in a managerial capacity before and in fact had never held a library position in any other organization. Don, however, had been counseling Bobby on his career and wanted him to have a chance to gain managerial experience. Bobby jumped into the interim role with zest, trying to be kind to everyone. He worked long hours himself, sending out orders quickly.

Staff all over the library soon became disenchanted with Bobby as wrong materials were received and accepted, items needed for reserve arrived late, and orders were generally slow to be processed. Bobby made sure requests from friends were placed quickly, however. Don saw the long hours Bobby was putting in and praised him for being so conscientious. Don insisted that the staff was being entirely too demanding and was not considering the difficulty of assuming an interim position.

When the vacancy was advertised, Bobby applied, but the search committee quickly eliminated him from consideration. When applicants were interviewed, the individuals liked by Don were the ones ignored or disliked by the staff.

****

Don's credibility was damaged when he continued to support Bobby despite the problems that arose. If he had worked with Bobby to correct the problems, the staff might have been forgiving. Instead, Bobby was not seriously considered for the job on a permanent basis and Don's evaluation of staff came into question. He was perceived as playing favorites or supporting those who were loyal to him. What better guidance could Don have given? How do managers avoid charges of favoritism?

The staff always assess the integrity and the straightforwardness of any administrator and will be quick to note fallibilities that surface. If a new manager is liked by the staff, errors in judgment and missteps will be forgiven initially, especially if the administrator is honest enough to admit them quickly. If an attempt to hide or deny them is made, and the staff observes this, credibility will suffer. Repeated judgment errors or misdirected cues will result in diminished credibility, especially if a pattern is noticed by staff.

Administrators can establish a high degree of credibility quickly by accurately analyzing the organizations for which they are responsible. This analysis, largely based on observation, can take several weeks or months to complete initially and should remain an ongoing process for fine tuning.

A part of the analysis is one-to-one communication and discussion with each member of the staff. This allows the manager to acquire an in-depth orientation of the entire organization or the segment for which he or she is responsible. Noting and storing verbal as well as nonverbal cues will allow the manager to detect patterns and possible problem areas necessitating changes.

As the one-to-one communication and orientation is underway, notes taken on site or afterwards while reviewing the discussions and hands-on experiences will prove invaluable for the next stage of the process. This next stage is drafting a formal, written assessment of the present situation, in effect creating a "white paper" of the strengths and weaknesses of the organization and the individual members of the staff, such as has been discussed in Chapter 1, "Laying the Groundwork for Change." This process will also detail the oral history of the library, determine the informal network and its leaders, and identify the potential targets of that network. This "white paper" will prioritize the problems and will lead to formulation of organizational goals, as well as formalizing the mission of the organization.

Sara Morgan had observed since she arrived at Simpson College to become library director that the head of reference, Marty Blake, was not performing effectively. As she queried the staff and learned the policies and procedures, she learned that Marty allowed friends to work the hours they wanted, had not bothered to train librarians newly arrived on staff, and tolerated a poor attitude toward patrons on the part of some staff.

Sara noted that Alice Trask, who had been at the college for almost as long as Marty, was looking for a job elsewhere. Alice had attempted to formalize the reference schedule and had offered to help new librarians learn the collection. She molified upset patrons whenever possible. However, Alice was very frustrated with Marty and had decided to go elsewhere.

One Monday following the weekend Marty was on duty, Sara received an irate call from a faculty member who was upset about Marty's treatment of students in one of his classes as they tried to do research for their term papers. This was not the first such incident, so she decided the time had come to demote Marty. She decided to place Alice in the head of reference position on an interim basis. She knew Alice had made efforts to correct the situation and the experience as head of reference would help her in applying for jobs elsewhere.

Over the next few months, Alice rearranged the reference desk schedule, visited with faculty, arranged tours of the library for students, and established required training plans for all staff. As the quality of service improved, letters of commendation were sent to Sara. The staff learned of these letters and took pride in what they had accomplished.

When the position was advertised, Alice was encouraged to apply by members of the reference staff. She was the top candidate recommended by the search committee and the staff evaluations. As a result, she was appointed head of reference permanently.

****

Is Marty an exception within the library profession? What chances did Sara take in demoting Marty and giving Alice the opportunity? Was Sara's timing right? How do good personnel decisions promote a manager's credibility? What constraints may a manager face in making such decisions and how can they be overcome?

Because she accurately perceived Alice's abilities and allowed Alice to make needed changes, Sara won the approval of the staff in general. She was perceived as being a good judge of people. The service mission of the library was successfully achieved and a new, effective manager was developed. Sara also achieved positive recognition for the library from the patrons.

ESTABLISHING OR REESTABLISHING CREDIBILITY WITHIN THE PARENT ORGANIZATION

Credibility within the library is not the only credibility that is important to a manager. He or she must also be recognized as an effective manager by colleagues and leaders of the parent organization and the institution's administration.

If a library is functioning well, the patrons will be generally pleased with the services received, and funding will be available. This does not necessarily mean that a high level of credibility exists but only recognizes the fact that the library is the information center and materials need to be acquired.

Administrative changes in the library or the parent organization require a period of readjustment on both sides and reestablishment of credibility among the key players. Input from the informal organization can again be very useful to a new library manager in determining what the parent organization's expectations of the library are and where previous administrators may have been lacking in meeting those expectations. Tests of outside credibility arise for a number of reasons: during normal budgetary negotiations; when "crises" arise because an influential patron finds services lacking or large numbers of patrons become exasperated with a library's decision that affects their use; and when financial difficulties arise, forcing the library to actively compete with other segments of the larger environment for shrinking funds.

If a new library manager has been straightforward with the administrators of the parent organization, apprising them of potential problems and sharing the constraints that exist, the administration will usually listen to explanations and allow time for the situation to be corrected. If a manager's credibility is low, however, the parent organization may use any unexpected problems to withdraw support or funding, leaving the administrator to be attacked by inside and outside forces. Managers of libraries in transition are especially vulnerable to some staff grievances and complaints by employees challenging new philosophies, changes, and expectations. If these grievances are handled correctly, according to established policies and involving all appropriate resources available, they can be used to explain to the parent organization the need for changes. Resolving grievances in an objective, rational manner can greatly enhance a manager's credibility and demonstrate effective human relations skills. The parent organization will usually watch carefully to see if an organizational equilibrium establishes itself after a given period of time. If staff dissatisfaction within the library continues to increase or grievances are mishandled, support for new managers is likely to be withdrawn and they may have to leave.

PLANNING FOR A NEW LIBRARY ENVIRONMENT

Effective planning efforts involve as many people as possible because individuals are more likely to implement decisions if they have had a part in their development. In managing organizations in transition, a successful planning process can be one of the first actions to convince employees that administrators and managers are serious about moving the library in new directions. If a library wants to broaden its administrative focus and move toward participative management, planning will be an excellent vehicle to put theory into practice. If done properly, planning requires that every kind of expertise in an organization be involved and consulted, without considering rigid lines of authority. Suggestions, recommendations, and ideas can flow freely from all parts of the organization. The formal organization structure needs to be involved only in the final stages to give authoritative approval.

Peter Drucker points out that progressive industries have learned that workers must be included in planning activities. "The worker himself, from the beginning, needs to be integrated as a resource into the planning process. From the beginning he has to share supervisors' thinking through work and process, tools and information. His knowledge, his experience, his needs are resources to the planning process. The worker needs to be a partner in it."[1]

In order to move successfully through a change process, library administrators need to understand the different phases of the change process and carefully plan for each stage.

Any change process can be placed along a time line. Three major stages can be identified. The primary purpose of the first stage is to evaluate the existing organization and its programs, to identify possible problems, and to generate alternative solutions.

During the second stage, a plan is developed and agreement sought to implement agreed upon solutions. Implementation of prioritized solutions follows.

During the third stage the success of the implemented actions is evaluated again and necessary adjustments of the actions may occur.

The initial phase of any change process benefits from involving as many people as possible to collect as much information as possible so that a library organization can examine a wide range of alternatives and gather data to assess their viability. Since the focus of this stage is collecting information, a flexible and open organizational arrangement encourages communication and establishes the fact that all individuals are valuable and that their ideas will be heard.

As information is collected, individuals at all levels can use the information to clarify the nature of the problems, and different forms of solutions will emerge. Some of these alternative solutions will be predictable and follow standard procedures. Others will be more innovative in nature. Still others will be whimsical and humorous. All should be welcomed and appreciated before being judged and evaluated.

In the second planning stage, the ideas are analyzed and evaluated. Each suggestion is scrutinized to assess its possible outcome and the possibility of implementation. The result of this scrutiny is the development of a plan for action. In many ways, this is the most important of all stages, for good planning will minimize error and speed actual implementation.

It is crucial that problems are properly defined and alternative strategies developed. Two procedures are essential in this process. The first is to evaluate possible outcomes of any alternative solution and to assess the significance of these outcomes. Questions raised at this stage should include:

- Are we pursuing a worthwhile goal?
- What are the short-range effects?
- What are the long-range effects?
- What units will be involved?
- What will be the short- and long-range effects on institutional resources?

The careful exploration of all possible or probable results from the change process will prevent any surprises from occurring in the later process of implementation and will keep energies focused on worthwhile outcomes during the planning stage.

Within the implementation phase there should be adequate testing of significant ideas for feasibility of implementation. Many worthwhile projects die before they begin because the resources for implementation are not at hand. Other times individuals abandon change projects altogether because they believe that they are impossible to implement.

In testing any idea for feasibility, a number of questions need to be considered:

- Is it possible to carry out this idea with existing resources?
- If not, can the resources be obtained from other areas?
- Specifically, what resources are necessary to carry out this plan?
- How much time (an important and often overlooked resource) will be involved?
- Having identified the resources necessary for implementation, can the persons who control these resources be identified?
- Are these people likely to be favorable to this idea?

Every plan then requires that others either approve or accept the idea in order for implementation to be successful. Organizations must consider these questions:

- What other people are going to be involved?
- Can the necessary resources be easily obtained? If not, can other avenues be explored?
- Have teams created an idea that requires the approval of a multitude of individuals? If so, how can the idea be revised so that fewer people would have to approve?
- Finally, how many individuals will be affected by this idea during the process of implementation? When will these individuals be informed of the idea? How will their acceptance be elicited? What procedures will be used to win their acceptance?

When questions about resources, approval, and acceptance of an idea have been satisfactorily answered, the idea is approaching becoming an actual plan. Selecting a strategy and drawing up a plan occur in the next stages of the process.

Much of the planning will evolve from having clearly evaluated the feasibility of the idea. If the feasibility of the project has been carefully explored, it is relatively easy to answer the following questions that must be confronted during this stage of the planning process:

- What steps need to be taken to implement this plan?
- Where in the time line of the plan must specific resources be acquired?
- When and how will the acceptance of other individuals who will be at least peripherally affected by the implementation of this plan be sought?

The answers to these questions will then outline the overall strategy for a proposed change project.

Now the specific planning stages follow. Specific steps must be outlined and placed along a time line. Individuals who will be accountable for accomplishing each step must be noted. Time must be allotted not only for implementing the steps themselves but for contacting all the individuals whose approval and acceptance will lead to the success of the proposed plan. Finally, as this substage concludes, those most centrally involved in the planning process must voice their commitment to the plan. Any objections or reservations should be brought to the surface so that the concluding plan will be supported by all involved in its design.

The last part of the planning process involves designing the specific measures by which progress toward goal completion will be evaluated.

- How will progress be measured? By whom? When?
- How will information flow through the entire group so that all central figures are aware of the progress of this project?
- Finally, what contingency measures are built in so that obstacles can be sidestepped when they occur?

With a time line of action steps, with responsibilities allocated, with feedback measures designed, and with contingency measures in place, the planning process is concluded and implementation can begin.

Organizational development studies show that there are certain common pitfalls to planning efforts. Awareness of these pitfalls or potential missteps will assist managers in avoiding planning and implementation problems or help with the analysis of why their own plans did not succeed.

1. Top management assumes that it can delegate the planning function to a planner.
2. Top management becomes too engrossed in current problems and doesn't spend sufficient time on long-range strategy problems.
3. The organization fails to develop goals suitable as a basis for formulating long-range plans.
4. Key personnel in line positions were not involved in the planning process.
5. Plans are not used as standards for measuring managerial performance.
6. Management fails to create or promote a climate that is congenial and not resistant to planning.
7. The organization assumes that comprehensive planning is something separate from the entirety.
8. So much formality is injected into the system that it lacks flexibility, looseness, simplicity, and creativity.
9. Top management fails to review with departmental and divisional heads the long-range plans that they have developed.

10. Top management consistently rejects the formal planning mechanism by making intuitive decisions that conflict with formal plans.

If all the stages are followed and adequate input is solicited, with individuals feeling committed to the change, the change process has a chance of success.

COMMON PROBLEMS

The change processes in organizations create technical, political, and cultural problems. Many managers think in terms of only one of these sets of problems. If technical problems are overemphasized, which is most likely in hierarchical organizations, the disregard exhibited for social and psychological factors will manifest itself in high absenteeism, low quality control, low productivity, and disinterest in the future of the organization.

Gerard Lemon had demonstrated an interest in learning preservation techniques and the archives managers supported him with time away from the workplace so he could acquire the necessary skills. When Gerard returned to the archives, he began to implement the techniques he had learned. Soon he had trained another employee in the basics. At the same time Gerard became romantically involved with a former coworker. He began to stay out late on week nights and as a result frequently came in late to work and often called in sick. Other employees in the archives saw that the employee Gerard had trained was doing most of the work while Gerard came and went as he wished. Animosity was directed toward Gerard by his coworkers; however, Gerard was unconcerned. Gerard's supervisor was reluctant to address the problem because he thought that Gerard would leave and the library would lose his skills.

****

Could Gerard's position and responsibilities have been better defined by the managers?

Gerard was concerned only with his own needs and felt little loyalty for the organization that had enabled him to meet some of those needs through acquisition of new skills and a certain amount of flexibility. Rather than recognizing that he had a responsibility to the organization, Gerard preferred to pursue an immature approach to the organizational needs. What can be done now to correct the situation? How would you as a manager address the problems created by Gerard's behavior?

A purely political emphasis on problem solving will create low levels of trust, cynicism, and win/lose strategies. Long-term organizational goals will be ignored, subverted, or lost under such conditions. In light of renewed interest in cultural or human problems within organizations, many managers may avoid dealing with the reality of power and technical change and want to build an organization solely on truth, trust, and love. They assume that all employees are reasonable and caring and will do the right thing if given an opportunity to choose. The most effective managers consider all dimensions when trying to understand and resolve the problems created by change.

James Sims, the library director, was impressed with Dorothy Knight's philosophy of participative management. When an opportunity for promotion presented itself, he promoted Dorothy, who had been a department head, to a senior administrative position. She began to assert herself with staff, trying to force them into new service programs that she knew were needed by patrons. James felt that since Dorothy was a very intelligent individual, she would see that force was not effective with a staff that did not yet understand the direction in which the library was moving. He placed his trust in Dorothy and expected the staff to do the same.

Over a period of several months, the staff became increasingly hostile. Dorothy responded by becoming more demanding. The new services were not proving effective. Finally James realized that an impasse had been reached and he was faced with either reassigning Dorothy or dealing with a staff in revolt.

****

Dorothy understood the philosophy of participative management but was inexperienced in implementing it. She saw the need for change and knew she had James' backing, so she tried to force new services to be incorporated into the library. James thought that by trusting Dorothy and allowing her to proceed everything would fall into place. He stepped back and she failed from lack of guidance. James had assumed that Dorothy would be reasonable and caring and would do the right thing. What steps can James take now? What are his options? How could James have determined if Dorothy actually practiced what she believed? What guidance should he have provided to her?

WORK ISSUES

Libraries in transition will find a variety of work issues surfacing and will need to address them as they arise. Many of these work issues will occur as a result of ongoing analysis of workflow and positions, an analysis that may be occurring for the first time within the organization.

Position Analysis

When new managers analyze staffing patterns, they often find that a disproportionate number of staff are employed in certain units. Options are to reassign staff to other units within the library where they might be more effectively used or to review all positions first. Involvement of the personnel department of the parent organization can add credibility and an objective perspective to this analysis.

Bridge positions can also be created, adding new functions and responsibilities to already existing jobs. While bridge positions are probably most easily created when vacancies occur, existing positions can also be redesigned or staff reassigned to positions that become bridge positions. The introduction of new programs into an organization is an ideal time to review positions and redesign existing or vacant positions.

As jobs are analyzed, supervisors may find that like tasks are being performed in several units and that the functions can be consolidated. Or supervisors may find that with changing work flow, it is valuable to have employees work in different functional areas, allowing them to develop new skills that will help them grow and that they can take with them when they decide to leave the organization.

Recruitment Criteria

With the redesign of positions and the creation of bridge positions, establishing different recruitment criteria for potential employees becomes necessary. These new criteria will include the ability to be flexible, to accept change, to learn a variety of tasks, to incorporate new philosophies into individual approaches to tasks, and to use automation without maintaining or creating parallel manual systems.

While recruiting new employees, managers can specifically look for these desirable traits. With existing employees, hired with different criteria and expectations, guidance and additional training will be needed.

As new programs are introduced, (such as end user database training and user instruction) and different approaches to collection development are incorporated into the organizational structure, training will be necessary for the current, as well as for newly hired, employees who may have not been exposed to such programs in previous organizations or in the classroom. In addition, there is a difference between learning theory and actual implementation.

Sensitivity to Staff Needs

As work issues surface, administrators in libraries in transition must be alert to stress points that may develop within the organization or with individuals. A reference staff formerly responsible only for providing assistance at the service point may suffer stress when responsibilities are changed, for example, with the addition of collection development or user instruction responsibilities.

Processing staff may react with anxiety when their jobs are broadened to include not only acquiring and processing materials but also providing assistance in use of these materials through assignment to staff service points. For a librarian suddenly expected to perform cataloging or reference tasks years after receiving initial training, the new expectations can be extremely stressful and may result in inappropriate behavioral reactions. A library manager who has had specific responsibilities for many years and who is now expected to use different approaches or to relinquish responsibilities for portions of the tasks to others may feel uncomfortable and experience a sense of being devalued. He or she may feel relegated to an inconsequential role, which may indeed be what has happened if he or she has been unwilling to incorporate the increased or changed expectations into a philosophy toward work.

NOTE

1. Peter F. Drucker, *Management: Tasks, Responsibilities, Practices.* New York: Harper & Row, 1975, p. 34.

PART II

Changing Organizational Roles

Chapter 4
The New Role Expectations

The typical library organization of the past was a hierarchy headed by a director and one or more other senior administrators. Titles varied and the number of organizational levels fluctuated, depending on the size of the library or library system. Within these organizations, the top administrative group was responsible for the development of the library's mission and goals, the implementation of policies, and the daily operation of the library.

Today libraries are experimenting with more flexible organizational structures. Academic libraries with faculty status for librarians are moving more and more toward the collegial system commonly used by their academic counterparts. Others may use subject rather than functional arrangements, where professionals use their subject expertise to develop the collection, catalog materials, and provide public service. Still other approaches include the incorporation of team management practices, parallel organizations, quality circles, or committees to make existing structures more responsive.

All of these measures are designed to provide employees with maximum input in decisions affecting their work and to use their talents to solve the complex problems faced by today's organizations. Administrators have concluded that they alone do not have all the answers; library staffs are eager to realize their beliefs that they have a major contribution to make beyond their daily activities.

The demand for accountability in all areas of public and private life has accelerated the need to broaden decision-making powers in all institutions. Organizational leaders under increasing scrutiny are much more eager to share their responsibilities; library staffs are educated and aware enough to grasp all opportunities for input.

THE ROLE OF SUPPORT STAFF

Because of library automation many activities previously considered as professional responsibilities are now being performed by support staff members. As a result librarians are being forced to redefine their positions and professional responsibilities while support staff often feel undervalued and underpaid.

Libraries appear to be blessed in their ability to attract highly educated and motivated staff for their nonprofessional positions. Many of these employees have at least an undergraduate degree; a small number have master's degrees and consider themselves as professional and as valuable to their departments as the librarians. Although salaries and responsibilities have generally increased for support staff, making their work more attractive and challenging, most libraries are locked into salary schedules prepared by parent institutions that often refuse to understand the value and complexity of the paraprofessional positions. Libraries, therefore, are having to deal with the tensions created by employing highly educated and to some extent overqualified personnel in clerical and support staff positions.

Those organizations that understand the dilemmas of their largely female support staff encourage the creation of an organizational climate that minimizes the division between professional and support staff members. Support staff are included in staff development activities, committees, task forces, and on search committees; their inclusion will provide them with opportunities to develop their skills, gain an overall perspective of the organization, and add to the decision-making process. Career counseling, internships, and scholarship programs can be used to provide opportunities for personal development to minimize the frustrations of being locked into a rigid personnel structure with few options for advancement and career progress.

As the library profession is again starting to experience shortages, support staff members who already have an undergraduate education and enjoy their work should be encouraged to pursue a professional library degree. Offering extension programs to those unable to leave their family responsibilities full time to attend a library school may be an attractive and practical solution for library schools in need of students, libraries in need of professional staff, and those support staff members who are suited for a career in librarianship.

As automation, business, personnel, and preservation functions in libraries become more specialized and distinct from the traditional collection development, bibliographic control, teaching, and public service functions of professional librarians, libraries will need to find an acceptable way to integrate these specialists, who are performing the new tasks, into the work force and the salary structure. Currently automation specialists are the most serious threat to the status and salary dilemmas of a predominantly female profession.

It is hoped that as information becomes more valuable and librarians' skills more in demand to interpret the multitude of available data, the existing salary differential between librarians and other library professionals will become an issue of the past. In the meantime developing and supporting the efforts of those already on the staff who have an interest in and talent for the emerging specializations will probably be the best course libraries can follow. This course will provide library and alternative career opportunities for existing staff and benefit the organization.

THE ROLE OF PROFESSIONAL STAFF

The claim of professionalism has been and appears to be a continuing issue for librarians. Because of the progressing automation of library functions and the increased need for information, the profession may be closer to defining those responsibilities that it considers truly professional.

Gould and Kolb define the term "profession" as "occupations which demand a highly specialized knowledge and skill acquired at least in part by courses of more or less theoretical nature and not by practice alone, tested by some form of examination either at a university or some other authorized institution, and conveying to the persons who possess them considerable authority in relation to 'clients'."[1]

Since society values professional status highly, librarians are not alone in identifying their work as a profession, continuously creating, refining, and redefining the necessary criteria to substantiate their claim. According to Shapero, professionals make up the largest single category in the work force in the United States; he attributes this category's growth to the need for specialists demanded by increased technology and the growing complexity of organizations. In addition a rising number of educated persons demand professional status for their work.[2] His list of those occupations classified as professions includes librarians together with doctors, architects, accountants, and engineers, among others.

The developing "Information Age" provides unique opportunities for librarians to practice and market their professional skill in and outside of libraries. Because of increased automation, fewer professionals are needed in traditional work assignments to perform those responsibilities previously considered professional. Those employed in libraries will perform the truly intellectual and managerial responsibilities necessary to acquire, classify, access, interpret, and retrieve information and leave the repetitive and more narrowly definable tasks to support personnel using automated processes.

The overwhelming volume of new information created each year will increase the demand for librarians to teach other professions and the public at large how to access and choose from among the multitude of facts. Because of a trend toward integration of knowledge from different fields, librarians will be forced to work in teams, pooling their subject expertise and bridging the gaps for specialized researchers. Their outreach and teaching functions are increasing to communicate to their "clients" the process necessary to access data needed to function in a complicated environment. They are the important link between information and user, a role requiring excellent communication and intellectual skills.

Since information storage is moving away from the book format, using computer technology instead, librarians have to become truly computer literate to assist patrons in overcoming their fears of technology and enabling them to use information available only in machine-readable data files.

As their evolving functions change the role of the library overall, librarians are forced to become more involved in internal organizational issues. They are demanding to be involved in redefining missions, establishing goals, allocating resources, coordinating colleagues, and delegating appropriate responsibilities to support personnel.

Librarians face tremendous personal and professional challenges to adequately perform all these responsibilities. If they succeed, the questions about professionalism can be laid to rest and they can move forward to take their esteemed place in society, a place which their expertise will justify.

THE ROLE OF MIDDLE MANAGEMENT

Middle managers are those individuals who are responsible for interpreting policies and procedures of the organization and overseeing their implementation. In addition they are accountable for the quality of services or production of work on a day-to-day basis. Because of current organizational development trends that advocate fewer levels of management, middle managers are often predicted to be a dying breed. Their frustrations, created by staff demanding more participation and top administrators holding onto their position power, are well documented and discussed.

Traditionally, middle management has been the training ground for executives. At this level, information about policies and procedures transmitted from the top is interpreted, operationalized, and enforced. If successful during these times of changing expectations, the current middle managers will be superbly trained to integrate the conflicting demands of the evolving library organizations at higher levels.

Much of their success will depend on their human relations and communication skills. Middle managers have to develop subordinates and involve them in the day-to-day management of the libraries so that they are able to understand and translate those overall library missions and policies that are set by top administrators into workable goals. Today, middle managers need to be able to encourage subordinates to be creative, articulate the need for change, and initiate action. Involvement of subordinates in decision making will develop essential trust relationships, which are based on mutual dependence, and will lead to better decisions, benefiting both the middle managers and the organization.

Insecure or inept middle managers in today's libraries will be unable to withstand the stresses and multitude of demands placed on their positions. If they feel threatened by a perceived loss of power as more employee participation appears to be a must, they will fail in developing their staff, with obvious disastrous results. If they are unable to work effectively with their organizational superiors, their understanding of the organizational change efforts will be lacking and make them incapable of leading an effective change process.

K. Kim Fisher has identified five stages in the development of participative systems, each providing unique challenges and requiring special roles and behaviors. The stages are:

1. Conception: In this stage the idea of either developing a new start-up participative work system or of changing an existing organization to a participative one is conceived. It typically involves a relatively small cadre of people and will generally produce a few 'charismatics' who will champion the concept through the early stages of work system development.

2. Incubation: In this stage the organization goes through the planning/designing and preparation required to successfully transform the organization. This is the stage for generating and demonstrating organizational support for the champion's vision.

3. Implementation: In the implementation stage the new work structures that are manifestations of the shift in the management paradigm are born. Changing or developing the job design; setting work rules; developing formal statements of work ethics/values, policies and procedures, and performance appraisal systems; forming 'core' or 'action communication teams,' and cross-functional problem-solving teams; and establishing flexible job descriptions, pay and promotion policies, skill development practices, information passing mechanisms, etc., occur.

4. Transition: The transition stage marks the 'completion' of implementation and the beginning of adjusting to and becoming competent in the new work system. The work teams themselves are growing so that they can take on the responsibilities required for maximum organizational effectiveness. Authority and autonomy transfers from higher to lower levels as skills warrant it.

5. Maturity: A key attribute of this 'final' stage is, ironically, that even though the work systems are 'completed' in the sense that they are fully functional, they continue from this stage forward to evolve and change. This is what Cherns (1977) calls incompleteness, or in other words, continuous improvement of the work unit. Analogously, though adults are chronologically mature, they continue to learn and change in response to things around them. Work units, like human beings who work in them, are never finished.[3]

According to Fisher, integrative middle managers have the following roles to play during the implementation of a participative management system:

Stage 1 - Conception: Managers complete participative transformation feasibility analysis; Support the real need for evolution; Champion participative management concepts; Line up commitment/resources for next stages; Determine appropriate timing for introduction.

Stage 2 - Incubation: Managers build trust; Demystify participative management/facilitate clarification; Articulate vision; Model participative behaviors; Ensure subordinate training and development; Facilitate "implications for us" analysis; Ensure that good communication processes are in place; Provide necessary resources.

Stage 3 - Implementation: Managers champion participative management system changes; Recognize success; Clarify roles/expectations.

Stage 4 - Transition: Managers encourage skill building and risk-taking; Transfer authority and autonomy to management teams as skills expand; Help people learn from mistakes; Provide protection from outside forces.

Stage 5 - Maturity: Managers facilitate continuous improvement; Lead system-wide changes; Provide skill development opportunities; Deal with destructive behavior.[4]

Competent middle managers in libraries are the key to successful organizational transformations. If they are unsuccessful in creating productive work teams and participative environments, they will block change and their departments or areas of responsibility will be out of sync with the rest of the organization, visible for all to see. Frustrations will build because of unfulfilled expectations and the middle manager will become increasingly ineffectual and isolated.

The acquisition department head at the Lincoln College library left to accept a promotion in another state. Clara Hopkins, who was in charge of the searching unit, was asked to take on the responsibilities until a new acquisition department head could be hired. Clara had been with the library for more than five years and had developed into a very capable librarian. She was in the process of completing a second master's degree and had earned the respect of colleagues for her expertise as a bibliographer. Clara also had many outside interests and was not part of any particular clique in the library; rather, she seemed to get along with everybody.

The Associate Director for Technical Services, John Parsons, liked Clara because she was always pleasant, a good worker, and never challenged his judgment, as some of the other librarians in Technical Processing had a habit of doing lately.

Clara eagerly accepted the responsibility as department head, thinking that she might apply for the position herself. Within a few days, however, problems started to develop. Staff, thinking that the time was right, requested some changes in procedures affecting workflow, which the previous department head had opposed. The library itself was in the process of changing, and staff in other areas of the library, under the direction of a new Associate Director of Public Services, were excited about the many new opportunities they were given to provide input and participate in the decision-making process. The acquisitions staff knew that the director, Anna Foreman, was very pleased with those changes and they hoped to finally be able to do their part to improve the efficiency of the library.

Clara went to John, asking for permission to make the changes proposed by her staff. John, whose background was in cataloging, saw no particular need for the changes and decided to test Clara's loyalty to him. He advised Clara to wait until a permanent head was appointed. Clara explained in the next staff meeting that John didn't think the time for the changes was right. Staff expressed their disappointment about John's foot dragging and again tried to convince Clara that the proposed changes would simplify work procedures and make the department more efficient. When Clara declined to proceed, staff members started to question her and John's general managerial skills and abilities.

Within a month after Clara took over as acting head, personality conflicts between several staff members in the department erupted openly and some employees refused to talk to each other. Clara, not trying to hurt anybody's feelings, would listen to each side, talk to John about it, but never took any action because John always said the staff would get over it.

Gradually, the work climate deteriorated to the point where staff members appeared to spend most of their time talking about each other and the shortcomings of Clara and John. Clara, who had been a candidate for the position of Head of Acquisitions, withdrew her application without any explanation and, when a new manager was hired, went back to her old responsibilities.

****

Why did Clara not succeed as Acting Department Head? What role did John Parsons play, if any, in her unsuccessful attempt to become an effective middle manager? Did the staff overreact to Clara's unwillingness to change workflow procedures?

It appears that Clara had never really analyzed what a department head's function was until she found herself in the acting position. John chose her as acting head because she would be loyal to him and not add to his difficulties, rather than because of any managerial abilities she might have.

Although the director was trying to bring about changes, it appears that the organization was moving unevenly in implementing changes. John Parsons appeared to be less able to implement changes than the other Associate Director, so the frustrations in Technical Processing seemed even more pronounced.

Clara may have proceeded by thoroughly analyzing the need for a change in work procedures, then writing a proposal for John, detailing all the benefits to be gained from the change. Instead, she felt insecure in her new role and looked to John for guidance. John appears to have been more concerned with asserting his position power than with developing his staff. A very real opportunity to use staff input and encourage creative thinking was ignored, giving the staff the message that their ideas did not count.

Since Clara refused to play the role of manager, leading the organization forward and encouraging creativity of staff, employees felt increasingly discouraged and turned their frustrations against each other. If Clara had seized the opportunity to bring about meaningful changes, she would have been able to build trust in the department and create a participative environment. The staff's enthusiasm and involvement could have produced many ideas to improve operations, with the credit reflecting on Clara and John.

THE ROLE OF ASSOCIATE/ASSISTANT DIRECTORS

The roles of associate/assistant directors are assuming more importance and relevance in libraries because library management is becoming more complex and directors have to spend an increasing amount of time on demands imposed from outside the organization.

Since directors can no longer make all the decisions, relationships between top administrators are evolving from a hierarchical to a team management approach. Associate/assistant directors are becoming responsible for the accomplishment of organizational goals, and in cooperation with the director, they plan, organize, motivate, and evaluate available resources, e.g., capital, people, equipment. Because of their knowledge of and involvement in the day-to-day operation of the library, associate/assistant directors have become the primary forces in transitional libraries to imbue staff with new philosophies, ideas and concepts, and to implement new technologies.

To function effectively in this expanded role, it is no longer appropriate to emulate the behavior of the library director, whose responsibilities may be more comparable to those of a chairperson of a board than those of a manager. Today's associate/assistant directors must develop effective managerial skills of their own and combine them with self-confidence, risk taking, and creativity.

At this organizational level three major competencies are essential:

1. Task-oriented skills, acquired through experience, education, and training.
2. Interpersonal skills, acquired by working with and through people.
3. Organizational knowledge—an understanding of organizations and their formal and informal structures.

While the appropriate mix of these skills or talents varies in different managerial positions, in a changing library organization all three are of primary importance to associate/assistant directors.

Often the first changes necessary are the result of the introduction of new technologies. If successfully implemented, they demand modifications of work procedures and organizational structures. Technical and organizational skills are essential to smooth adaptation by staff and to develop higher levels of professionalism and competencies.

To obtain a genuine commitment for changes from subordinates, peers, and superiors, effective associate/assistant directors must develop and exercise excellent human relations skills. Management research indicates the ability to get along with people is the most important single skill of an executive. It is more vital than intelligence, decisiveness, knowledge, or job skills. Good human relations skills will allow associate/assistant directors to exercise personal and position power wisely, to provide and withhold rewards, to be responsive to people's needs, and to invite subordinates to participate in decision making, all measures necessary to facilitate the change process.

Effective library directors will delegate as much authority as possible to the most technically knowledgeable level to make the organization more responsive, effect quicker responses, and develop leadership abilities in subordinates. At the associate/assistant director level, decisions to be made are of major importance and critical to the organization. The ability to make independent decisions is therefore essential to managers at this level. The library director is less likely to be around to be consulted and has in part hired associate/assistant directors to make those decisions that previously may have been his or her prerogative. The more a manager at this level perceives a need to check every decision with the "boss," the more this suggests a lack of ability, initiative, and self-confidence. When managers consistently fail to accept responsibility, misread organizational goals, or create disruptive environments because of a lack of skills, the library director must intervene by requiring additional training, reassignment, or even termination. Such actions divert the director's attention from his responsibilities to interact with the greater environment to secure much needed support and resources.

Successful associate/assistant directors will establish trust relationships with all levels in the organization. Without them, the creative innovations and risks necessary to implement changes will not occur. Successful associate/assistant directors will model new organizational behaviors with the support of the library director. They will demonstrate and encourage acceptance of divergent opinions and actions because it will foster creativity and progress.

Associate/assistant directors are the most accessible and visible members of top management. If they espouse new values and participative management ideas but fail to implement them in their areas of responsibility, the change momentum of the organization will come to a halt. The differences between what they say and how they act will be used by the more conservative staff members to discredit change efforts and undermine the fragile trust relationships building among all organizational segments.

As staff competencies are recognized and developed, associate/ assistant directors also need to transfer and delegate as much authority as possible to enable middle managers to understand the greater organizational concerns and enable them to be accepted into mutually beneficial partnerships.

Managers who are likely to fail at the associate/assistant director level are often characterized by the following:

1. The person moved into the position too quickly without acquiring the necessary technical, interpersonal, and organizational skills at a lower managerial level.
2. The person lacks interpersonal credibility and is unable to establish trust relationships with part of the organization.
3. The person has a trail of unresolved or ineffectually handled problems at lower levels but usually leaves an organization before the consequences of these actions become visible.
4. The person was habitually "saved" from disaster by a director, but he or she has now departed or no longer chooses to intervene when problems implement.

After a long search the Public Library of Circle City hired a new Associate Director for Technical Services, Walter Cayre. Walter emerged as the leading applicant after his two-day interview because the staff of the entire library was in agreement with his management philosophy. He believed in participative management and told them how he would work *with* the people who reported to him by establishing committees, task forces, and parallel organizational structures.

Not only was Walter sharing their philosophy, staff reported happily, but he was also handsome, witty, and very cosmopolitan. Everybody was excited to have had such a successful search and an air of anticipation hung over the entire library on the day of Walter's arrival.

The library director, Paul Beerman, was pleased with the new associate director and his approach to management. He knew that Walter would make a good impression on the community and provide a good role model for the staff. He had talked to Walter about the need to streamline the Technical Processing area in the aftermath of automation so that limited resources could be shifted to those new services demanded by the public. Walter was very articulate and emphatic in his understanding of the library's problem and indicated his enthusiasm for making the necessary changes.

After several months working long hours on his new job, Walter offered to release several of the professional catalogers to other areas, since most of the cataloging was now accomplished by using a major utility. Among those catalogers Walter offered to release was Rita Cooper, who was the Assistant Head of Cataloging and had been with the library for almost 15 years. She was well-liked and respected in the library. Some had actually encouraged her to apply for Walter's position, but Rita had other priorities in her life at the time and did not feel like taking on the additional responsibilities of an associate directorship. The Head of Cataloging was in her late 50s and still in good health. Rita saw herself moving into that position as the time came. Walter, on the other hand, believed that by eliminating an Assistant Head position the department would become less hierarchical in organizational structure and Rita's standing in the community might be helpful in the development of the new programs that library director Beerman was hoping to implement.

When Walter talked to Rita about a transfer he told her that there were too many catalogers in the department and that her talents could be better used in the Public Service area. Rita was stunned. She conferred with trusted colleagues about her dilemma and decided to tell Walter that she had thought about eventually becoming the Head of Cataloging and she didn't want to change her career direction. Walter became angry and told Rita that she was inflexible and uncooperative and if that was her attitude, she certainly was not going to become Head of Cataloging.

Walter apprised Beerman of the conflict. Beerman believed Walter's story that Rita was stubborn and inflexible and had only her own interests at heart. Walter used that support to give Rita a bad evaluation as the year ended, especially marking her down on her attitude. He realized that most people in his division supported Rita, and he decided through the evaluations to show everybody what he thought of their uncooperative attitude. During the evaluation process the department was in uproar. Although the incidents Walter used to support his view of their professional shortcomings were objectively correct, staff members felt that Walter had concentrated only on their shortcomings and chose to overlook their positive contributions.

Walter was surprised when *his* evaluation from the staff came up six months later. They found him dictatorial, unable to communicate, vindictive, and lacking basic managerial skills. Walter left Circle City within a year. He felt very hurt and could never understand why the staff had turned on him.

****

What could Walter have done differently? His intentions were good. Was Rita right in refusing a transfer? What went wrong with the evaluations? Was the staff right in "retaliating" and giving Walter such a bad evaluation? Could he have made a fresh start?

Walter failed to analyze and take into account the strength and power of informal leaders like Rita. Instead of using Rita's trust relationships with the staff to help bring about necessary changes, he perceived her as a threat and tried to minimize her influence in his division. Through his actions, Walter united the entire division and library staff against him on Rita's behalf and he, as the newcomer, lost.

Although Walter, for a time, had the backing of Beerman, he failed to develop trust relationships with all parts of the organization, and as a result, he failed in the position. If peers or subordinates do not trust a manager, they will find ways and means to sabotage important projects, fail to communicate essential information, and wait for the right opportunity to make him or her look so bad that even the superior has to notice. In Walter's case, the evaluations he wanted to use to consolidate and exercise his power were used by the staff as evidence of lacking interpersonal relations skills.

In many libraries the role of associate/assistant directors is becoming more specialized. Traditionally associate/assistant directors were considered the deputies of the director and could perform his or her responsibilities when necessary; today that is not always true. While there appears to be a trend and need to create deputy director positions with responsibilities for internal operations of the libraries, there is at the same time a trend to create positions for specialized and definable functions like budgeting, personnel, development, building services, and computer systems operations, to name just a few. Often these staff positions carry associate/assistant director titles. All of these positions have librarywide responsibilities and have taken on parts of responsibilities previously performed by the directors. Their influence and effectiveness depends in part on the library's needs and the value assigned by the director to their particular area of expertise.

In times of budgetary constraints, the expertise of a development person may greatly enhance a library's viability, while at the time of the introduction of an online catalog, the incumbent in a systems position may play the most critical role within an organization. Although budgeting, personnel, and facilities issues are continuous parts of organizational lives, they gain more prominence in times of transition, when organizational resources are being reexamined and reallocated. These roles offer excellent career opportunities for librarians with talents or backgrounds in those specialized areas.

THE ROLE OF THE DIRECTOR

The director of a library remains the primary leader in the organization and the main representative to the outside. He or she carries the ultimate responsibility for expenditures of allocated funds, effective provision of services to patrons, and staff performance of assigned duties.

In decades past, it was not uncommon for the library director to be someone who determined acquisitions for the collection, managed the daily operation of the library, and personally selected staff at all levels. The director was not only the leader but also the chief manager. This all-encompassing role is still played by many directors of smaller libraries with limited staffs.

Arnold Smith is director of the Waterford College library in rural Illinois. He has a professional staff of seven and a support staff of 15.

The library serves a college community of 5,000 students who are mostly from the region. Enrollment includes a number of foreign students. Almost all of the library staff members were born and raised in the town of Waterford, where the college is located. Most professionals got their degree at the state university about 200 miles away, after which they came back to their hometown. The staff is unionized and highly paid. Most have been with the library for 15 years or more. Two professionals were "given" to the library after they failed to be tenured in the College of Education and the Department of English. Neither possesses a library degree or sees a need to acquire one.

Arnold was hired from outside, following the firing of the previous director after a two-year tenure. The union had proven that he was unable to communicate with his staff. Arnold considers himself highly professional. This is his first directorship and he is determined to bring many positive changes to the library and develop its staff.

After several months on the job, Arnold realizes that his staff operates with limited, outdated skills and feels threatened by his high expectations. A staff member who is about to leave alerts him that a grievance will be filed by the former English professor, charging Arnold, too, with a lack of communication. Arnold feels angry and isolated. The person who hired him left shortly after he arrived, so he now reports to a vice-president for academic affairs whose judgment he doesn't trust and who is known for his inability to make decisions.

Arnold decides to throw himself into his work. He analyzes all positions, changes workflow and procedures, and introduces new library services, hoping his staff will learn from his good example and grow into their new responsibilities.

After two months the staff goes on strike and Arnold's boss advises him to look for another position within the next year.

****

Were Arnold's expectations about developing his staff realistic? What could he have done differently? Would you want to be the next director at Waterford College? If chosen, how would you proceed?

Arnold judged his staff according to his own standards of professionalism and motivation. He thought that professionals would be eager to learn and develop and be excited by the changes in the profession. The staff at Waterford College, on the other hand, was comfortable and pleased with the status they had achieved within their community. They thought that they did a fine job and saw no need for the drastic changes Arnold imposed. They resented his interference in all their work procedures and felt put down by his attitude of knowing everything better. The more Arnold became involved in their daily activities, the less time he had to keep in contact with other library directors. He had no peer group with whom he could discuss problems and gain a different perspective.

The person to whom he reported was of little help. Arnold should have delegated much of his work analysis and resulting procedural changes to staff members to develop their skills. He could have sent librarians to professional association meetings and had them report back upon their return. Those willing to develop could have received extra rewards and much positive feedback, leading the way for other change efforts. Arnold himself should have built his network of peers, asking for advice on how to handle particular situations and making himself as marketable as possible, to enable him to find another position in a less isolated library.

As libraries evolve into more complex organizations, the directors become more involved in external activities and are forced to relinquish some of their decision-making authority. A management structure has to be created to deal with the day-to-day operation of the library and permit business to continue as usual.

Library directors who are comfortable with a centralized and authoritarian managerial approach are being overwhelmed by the diversified needs of their positions. Those who are desperately holding onto their power bases are becoming more frustrated and ineffective because they are unable to fulfill the expectations of their superiors and staffs. Most directors have grown with the demands of their positions. Out of sheer self-preservation they have kept abreast of the changing needs of organizations in general and libraries in particular. To keep up with the demand of their positions they feel forced to experiment with new management techniques.

As library directors move from an authoritarian, to a participatory, to a consultative, to a team leadership approach, they will need to internalize the values of these management philosophies and instill them in those who report to them. To make a successful transition, library directors must feel very secure with their own abilities and the abilities of their colleagues as delegation becomes the rule rather than the exception.

The leadership qualities of chief executive officers are receiving renewed interest and recognition in the management literature, demonstrating that the most important role of library directors is the role of leader within the parent organization and the library itself. For some traditional directors, who feel more comfortable with the day-to-day activities, assumption of the leadership role may be very difficult and stressful.

Because directors are the main contact persons with the larger environment, they must be sensitive and adjust when that environment changes. Their role is to constantly monitor outside influences, build coalitions and support for the library, and educate staff about opportunities available and constraints imposed by the outside world. They must mentor the associate/assistant directors who report to them in the art of administration and representation.

Berta Bowers became the library director of the satellite campus of a major state university in Texas. She did an excellent job in developing a library from scratch to support the programs offered. Her relationship with the campus president was excellent. He admired her drive, energy, and ability to get things done. Under Berta's leadership, the library moved three times, each time into bigger facilities. She had a reputation as a go-getter.

The growth of the satellite campus plateaued at about 5,000 students and its funding stabilized. The university president was promoted to a more important position within the university system. Although the library continued to grow, it never reached the rate of expansion of the previous years.

Berta persisted in requesting large budget increases each year, which were patiently but consistently turned down by the new president. She became increasingly dictatorial with her staff and started to suffer from severe periods of depression. Her staff, who had built the library with her, became increasingly concerned and discouraged. After Berta failed once again to get the requested library budget, she made a scene in front of the president's office and had to be placed on leave for an indefinite period of time. Although she visited her library often during the following months, giving orders to staff so that the organization would not fall apart during her period of illness, Berta never came back as director. She retired for health reasons.

****

Berta failed to adjust to the changing expectations and different administration. Besides administrative changes, what are some other clues Berta had to indicate a changing environment? Do you believe that some administrators are more suited than others to manage a library during certain phases in a library's history?

Today effective library directors must be as flexible as their staffs and adept at making changes in their managerial styles. They must explore different organizational structures because they know that their institutions are organic and evolving and not stable, unchanging, static worlds. Library managers now find it necessary to adopt techniques that have been proven effective in other organizations. Librarians eager to move forward will look toward their directors to lead their institutions and the profession into the future. If the director lacks vision, the organization will wither. If the leadership role is not comfortable for him or her, someone else within the organization will in effect become the organizational leader and conflict will inevitably arise.

As a result of the positions they occupy, library directors have authority. The scope of their authority is defined by the organization but the extent to which it is used is at the discretion of the library director.

Directors will also need to exercise personal power as reflected in expertise, credentials, and personal attributes. Persons leading through position authority and personal power have a high potential of being effective directors. Skill in how and when to use each will determine the level of success in the position.

When a new director takes over the leadership role in a library, his or her acceptance will initially depend on how he or she was selected for the position. If the selection process was perceived as ethical, properly administered, and consistent with the standards of the organization, directors will be accepted and their legitimacy not questioned.

The director of the Pleasant Valley Public Library retired after 35 years in the position. For years the Assistant Director, Clare Beauford, was his right hand. The staff's opinions about Clare's competencies were sharply divided. She inspired fierce loyalty in about half the employees, while the other half thought she was only marginally competent and had obtained her position because of her connections within the community.

Clare was appointed acting director of the library while a search was conducted for a replacement. Library staff carefully watched appointments to the search committee to see if the committee was "stacked" with Clare supporters. Everything appeared to be fair and above board.

Unexpectedly, the region where Pleasant Valley was located went into a depression because of a major coal strike which everybody expected to last for months. The economic impact on the city was soon felt and the city manager, intent on saving money, called off the search for a new library director and permanently appointed Clare to the position. Within a year, half of the staff had left and with economic conditions worsening, most could not be replaced. Even those who had long supported Clare started to blame her for the library's low morale and high turnover. The city manager wondered if he had made the right decision in making the permanent appointment.

****

How would you respond to the city manager's doubts? Is Clare Beauford a victim of circumstances? How could her problems have been avoided?

Acceptable directors must appear confident, have the required educational credentials, have demonstrated knowledge and experience, and be reliable sources of information and advice. Directors may, of course, control information and, therefore, make it impossible for anyone but themselves to make informed decisions. Directors' interpretations of organizational situations are also a way to exert control. If a director does not objectively evaluate organizational problems, the problems may be minimized and ignored or maximized and dealt with too severely. Consistent misuse of authority or demonstrated incompetence will necessarily lead to diminished status and loss of legitimate authority. How a director treats subordinates also helps to determine the amount of actual power he or she controls and dispenses. Does he or she treat staff with dignity and respect?

Individuals in most organizations often find themselves in leadership roles without having acquired all the needed skills. This is also true for libraries. Librarians often attain a responsible position through appropriate credentials or as a reward for past achievements, but if the managerial skills are not in place, leadership will not come with the position.

There is a heightened sensitivity of employees toward leaders who misuse their positions. Administrators today must operate at a stricter level of accountability or their positions and power will be vigorously challenged with allegations of unethical conduct. The misuse of position and power is unethical behavior and may result from a lack of ethics, failure to plan, or lack of consideration of long-term effects. Employees are very aware when administrators represent their own needs as the organization's needs, a self-gratifying action that will ultimately be destructive to self and others as well as to the organization. Integrity is critical to directors who wish to also be the organizational leaders.

Bernard Fischer was library director at the Technical Institute in Mountain Ridge. He was a very attractive and charming man, and his staff was proud of his reputation within the state. He had built an excellent library during the 10 years of his leadership and was active in professional organizations and the community.

Bernard enjoyed travelling and during the first years of his tenure often took a few days of vacation in conjunction with his travels to professional meetings around the country. Lately the staff noticed that Bernard took lengthy trips to other continents on business. They were proud that he was such a well-known authority on automation that his services were requested worldwide.

Bernard's administrative assistant left for another position shortly after he returned from one of his trips. Before she quit she confided to a library friend that Bernard's trips were not paid for by the foreign libraries but that the travel was financed out of a special library fund that was to be used for staff development. She knew that he always stayed at very expensive hotels and travelled first class because she processed his travel claims.

The staff member she confided in, Louise Ramos, was shocked and refused to believe it. She had asked many times for permission to go to conferences, and like others, she had been told that there were insufficient funds available for such activities.

Louise had a cousin who worked in the budget office. After several weeks, Louise asked her cousin if there was a special fund for staff development for the library. Her cousin confirmed that and mentioned that it came from the endowment of a benefactor, who had set up the fund years ago. The interest amounted to almost $15,000 a year. She told Louise she had always wondered why it was only used by Bernard Fischer but felt it wasn't her responsibility to question it since his travel was always approved by the budget officer. Louise kept the information to herself until it was time for the annual state library conference. When several people were turned down because of lacking funds, she told them about the special fund.

Library staff started to question other expenditures Bernard had made that they thought benefited him personally. They remembered that he had purchased an expensive stereo system for his office from maintenance and operating funds. After a few months he had taken it home to work on it; he had never brought it back. Before long, Bernard noticed that his staff appeared rather cool toward him, but he wasn't concerned. He left to start his own consulting business after an audit of his travel expenses was performed.

****

Why was Bernard able to behave unethically over an extended time period? Don't all employees misuse library resources to some extent? Where do administrators draw the line? What could staff have done in the situation with Bernard?

Library directors have a lot of authority—often sole authority for how accounts are expended. Abuse of authority can go unquestioned for a long time.

Leaders, besides being ethical, must also be emotionally mature. They must cope with varied and unexpected pressures in a levelheaded, calm manner, using reliable judgment and making decisions for the good of the organization, not for personal gratification. They must relate well to others and have a genuine concern for staff because the success of any organization depends on its employees. Consideration for individual needs, however, cannot impair the striving for the achievement of overall organizational goals or obscure present and future organizational goals. Leadership implies responsibility for one's actions.

While position power is strengthened when the leaders deal with critical situations in a rational manner, personal power can easily be destroyed by contradictory or emotional behavior. Once the power and trust are lost, they are virtually impossible to regain.

Leaders in libraries depend on excellent interpersonal relations skills for success. They must communicate openly with others, even those whom they know disagree with their philosophies and methods. Employees today spend the majority of their waking hours at work and expect to be treated with genuine concern for their well-being. They are not machines; they know that the success of an organization depends on their cooperation. Employees consider themselves to be partners of management and will resist any manager who treats them without respect or tries to manipulate them.

There appears to be a fine line between respecting employees and laissez-faire management. Employees expect a certain measure of control from management, but the reasons for exerting it need to be communicated. If individual needs are the only concern of managers, productivity will suffer and everybody will lose in the process. Achieving a fine balance between employees' and organizational needs is the goal of excellent directors.

Directors above all can solidify—or weaken—their leadership role through the decision-making process. Basically there are four ways for directors to make decisions: centralized, consultative, consensus, and delegation.

1. The style most common in the past was centralized and when carried to extremes, this style became autocratic or dictatorial. This approach to making decisions did not allow for the development of other decision makers within an organization and led to a consolidation of power. Many library organizations today suffer the consequences of this style since the leaders have retired or are retiring after long tenures without having developed the necessary decision-making skills in staff within their organizations.
2. Progressive directors have adopted styles in which decisions are made after consultation. Input is solicited, but the actual decision making is still centralized. For most organizations, it is appropriate for some decisions to be made in this manner.
3. Some decisions may also be made through group consensus with the director assuming no more authority than the rest of the group. These techniques, although helpful for brainstorming activities, may also lead eventually to "group think" and decisions that lack a high level of quality.
4. Finally, decisions may be made after authority is delegated to subordinates within defined limits.

Lack of skill in using the latter three decision-making styles may make centralized decision making through autocracy appear preferable for the organization. The effective leader will use each technique upon occasion. For example, some time-pressured situations will require centralized decision making with no input. On occasion some decisions should be made centrally simply because they are not worth the time involvement of the entire group. Generally a library faces all kinds of decisions each day and it is the director's responsibility to develop decision-making skills in all employees.

The directors who are leaders know they are dependent on those they lead for their own success. Thus, a key element in being a leader is building leadership skills in others.

NOTES

1. J. Gould and William Kolb, *A Dictionary of the Social Sciences.* New York: The Free Press, 1964, p. 542.

2. Albert Shapero, *Managing Professional People.* New York: The Free Press, 1985.

3. K. Kim Fisher, "Management Roles in the Implementation or Participative Management Systems," *Human Resource Management* 25 (Fall 1986): 461–62.

4. Fisher, p. 468.

Chapter 5
Managerial Requirements
for Changing Organizational
Roles

Libraries in transition require unique managerial abilities and skills in order to move from a traditional control-oriented to a value-driven organization. Needed are caring, creative, flexible, and visionary managers who can function well in a multidimensional environment without the assistance of tried-and-true methods.

After decades of high expectations, dwindling resources, low credibility of authority figures, and little hope for the future, employees are becoming increasingly determined to take control over their own lives and to collectively guide the organizations in which they spend most of their energies.

MORAL LEADERSHIP

Effective managers today will have to be role models and demonstrate the new values and beliefs embraced by library employees. Needed, above all, is moral leadership in action to inspire the trust necessary to move the organization and its human resources toward new visions. The time when positional authority created automatic respect is gone. Managers today have to earn the respect of their employees by working for the common good, instead of solely for their individual or career goals.

Smart managers know that the only way to be successful today is to share the recognition with the people who made it possible through their efforts. Those unwilling to admit their dependence on the goodwill of the people they supervise will ultimately fail in their efforts to achieve success. The myth of the self-made man or woman is slowly being replaced by the realization that those working well in groups have a better chance of achieving successful careers and lives.

Managers and leaders of the '80s and '90s must be able to embody and demonstrate the new values. This requires an understanding of the changing beliefs and attitudes of the work force and an agreement that these changes are for the better. Because these leaders are usually chosen for their insights and expertise concerning the motivation of the contemporary employee, it is likely that they have experienced themselves the hopes and frustrations felt by the people they now manage. They probably know how it feels to not be consulted about work matters affecting their lives, not to have input in decision making, not to be valued as an intelligent human being able to make a contribution, and they have chosen to help bring about the necessary changes.

COURAGE AND RISK TAKING

Managers in libraries in transition must have courage and take risks because their visions and values will be continuously tested by the skeptics and those who have been disappointed too many times. Creative and new endeavors have always been subject to ridicule and predictions of doom. Those benefiting from the status quo are eagerly waiting to attack the untried and unproven. Successful managers will therefore have a high tolerance level for ambiguity, failure, and frustration combined with a strong sense of purpose, self-confidence, and unselfishness.

In all likelihood, they have experienced failure before and learned from it. Although they remember the pain, they cherish the insights gained and know that failures are temporary. They realize that setbacks make excellent teachers and force people to grow. As managers, they therefore don't keep employees from making mistakes. Rather, they put mistakes into the proper perspective and assist in analyzing what went wrong and what can be learned from the experience.

Managers must have the courage to communicate their convictions, to have them challenged and to adjust them, if necessary. Although his or her values and beliefs may be correct, a manager must take into consideration the maturity and ability of those he or she leads before making timely changes. This approach requires patience with people, respect for their individuality, and confidence that the vast majority of employees are able to and want to grow.

An important facet of courage is a willingness to take risks, to try something different, to have faith in the creativity or ability of coworkers and subordinates. It does not mean to forge ahead blindly without considering the likely consequences. Before taking a major risk, a good manager will:

- analyze the situation carefully
- analyze staff strengths and weaknesses and determine how to most effectively use both

- judge the attitude of the institutional administration to determine if there is enough trust and willingness to back a new approach
- carefully plan a strategy for the proposed change, building in alternatives
- question colleagues in other libraries that have undergone similar changes about the pitfalls and successes to anticipate
- be comfortable with the direction in which the risk-taking will lead
- know where the support—and opposition—will likely come from and how to maximize the former and minimize the latter
- analyze the possible consequences should the risk-taking fail and determine if the organization and the manager can live with those consequences

Successful risk-taking on the part of managers will lead to risk-taking on the part of staff. If a risk fails, the staff must observe that the failure is viewed by management as a learning experience, not as an offense for which the "offender" must be punished. If a pattern is developed in which successful risks are rewarded and failed risks are used as learning experiences, the library employees will become more creative, suggest changes, and support the efforts of others.

Again, management must be the first to take risks and demonstrate support. It is essential that managers admit failure, analyze why failure occurred, learn from it, teach staff how to build on failure, apologize publicly and sincerely if the failed risk hurt someone, and move forward despite the failure, rather than being paralyzed by fear.

TRUST

Managers of today's organizations must be able to inspire trust in the future of the organization and thereby build commitment, loyalty, competence, creativity, and belief in the organizational mission. Building on the organizational history, both good and bad, managers need to create a sense of cohesion and a road map for the future. As a result employees will feel that their contributions are valuable and that their place in the organization is secure. Once their "safety" needs are taken care of, they can then devote energy to deal with the ambiguities of changing organizational structures, policies, procedures, and managerial practices.

In many transitional library organizations management will spend the first year or longer in rebuilding trust. This process requires first of all a belief that employees, if given a choice, will want to do the right thing. Second, patient efforts must be made to enable subordinates to acquire the necessary skills for participative management. Next, opportunities must be provided to practice the newly acquired skills. Employees willing to change want to be given recognition for their efforts and achievement; at the same time they need reassurances that they are proceeding in the desired direction. Managers themselves need to develop their own skills continuously and be open to a questioning attitude from their employees.

Rebuilding trust is a time-consuming and sometimes disheartening process. Although employees usually are willing to give new managers the benefit of the doubt, they will be watching most intensely to discern patterns of behavior. Managers are aware that it is easy for a group of employees to fashion an accurate and complete picture of a manager's strengths and weaknesses in a relatively short time, since they will share their observations with each other. Employees will not expect perfection. Rather they will value honesty, a good sense of humor, integrity, and, above all, a willingness to admit one's fallibilities. It will make them feel less threatened and more comfortable to realize that a manager knows his or her own weaknesses and is not afraid to admit them and overcome them. They can then allow themselves to also be open, instead of covering up mistakes and blaming others.

Nevertheless, setbacks are inevitable. Although employees may be intellectually convinced that the changes are good for the organization and their own well being, sometimes they may feel stressed by the many unknowns and fall back into familiar old behavior or work patterns. A manager who wants to build trust reassures constantly that things will be better and that it is normal to feel hesitation and even fear during the change process. Pointing to successes and expressing faith in the employees' abilities, will move most skeptics forward again.

SELF-AWARENESS

In transitional organizations everything is fluid and managers cannot rely on established policies and procedures to back their decisions. They must trust their own instincts and experiences to decide when the time is right to proceed, retreat, or wait for other developments. No matter how well changes are planned and how highly motivated staff is, unexpected interventions from inside or outside the organization will always require adjustments of timetables and goals. A strong belief in one's own ability and faith in the ability of others will help in overcoming any unforeseen obstacles. Viewing the change process itself as a worthwhile learning experience rather than simply as a means to achieve an end will help managers remain focused on the overall goals.

Richard L. Schott speculates that the quality and capacity of today's managers may well depend on the extent to which they have successfully mastered the developmental tasks of adult life. Good management, according to him, is based on, among other things, a capacity for empathy and the ability to define where an individual is "at" in terms of his or her needs and motivations. A manager who is unaware of his or her own growth patterns and developmental tasks may very well be impaired in judging others. A manager who is more highly "evolved" developmentally is likely to be more effective in dealing with superiors, colleagues, and subordinates.[1]

Schott partially bases his conclusions on the research of psychiatrist Michael Maccoby, who suggests that today's leaders are less egocentric and narcissistic than their predecessors, somewhat less inner-directed, and more other-directed. These individuals display such traits as tolerance, flexibility, and a willingness to experiment with new relationships at home and in the family. At best, the new character is playful and oriented to self-development and the development of others, in terms of health, life-long learning, adventure, and enriching experiences.[2]

Maccoby describes the new leaders as imbued with "a caring, respectful and responsible attitude; flexibility about people and organization structure; a participative approach to management; and the willingness to share power. Furthermore, they are self-aware, conscious of their weaknesses as well as strengths, and concerned with self-development for themselves as well as others." [3]

These characteristics suggest that those leaders have experienced and overcome the major developmental tasks of their lives and are now able to draw on their own experiences to understand and guide others.

Natalie Sage was a reference librarian at Holt University. This was her first position after graduating from library school; she had moved from another state to accept the job. During her first year Natalie was pleased and excited about being a professional. She had an excellent attitude about her job and its responsibilities.

Shortly after returning from her vacation to start the second year, Natalie had a disagreement with one of her older colleagues. Natalie felt that the suggestions she had made to improve the computer search process had been totally ignored and that her opinions had not been taken seriously. She started to feel unappreciated and wondered if she had been wise to come to Holt University. In the course of talking to several of her younger colleagues she noted that all had something they didn't like about their jobs, which confirmed her opinion that the Holt University library was not a good place to work. Natalie's attitude deteriorated. She started to be absent frequently, and when asked to give her opinion in meetings, she never said a word.

Her supervisor, Gail Brock, was concerned about Natalie and tried to find out in informal and formal meetings what was wrong. Natalie would just say she wasn't feeling well but that nothing was seriously wrong. She indicated that she needed to work some things out, but Gail was not to worry about it because it really didn't matter.

When Natalie's absenteeism started to affect the morale of the entire department, Gail once again had a frank talk with Natalie and told her how her attitude and frequent absences were affecting everybody's work. Then Gail proceeded to tell Natalie that she had gone through a similar experience at the beginning of her career, when she realized that all her ambitions and dreams would not materialize overnight. Gail also told Natalie that it was normal to experience a reality shock after starting to work because unrealistic expectations about one's impact on the organization and the world were usually not fulfilled. Gail offered to work with Natalie to see where her area of responsibility could be increased and to help her through this difficult time. She hoped that Natalie would not leave because she suspected that the same disappointment would set in at a different place. Gail discussed how Natalie's career might progress at Holt University and told her she would be very marketable if she stayed two to three more years.

After several conferences, Natalie's outlook and attitude seemed to return to normal and her productivity increased, while her absenteeism decreased.

****

What was the key to Gail's success with Natalie? Can managers expect variations of commitment to a library during a person's career? When do you think career satisfaction may be at a peak?

Manfred Kets de Vries and his associates suggest a strong relationship between job satisfaction and phases in a person's lifespan development. According to their research individuals can expect:

1. Reality shock during their twenties. As a result organizational commitment and career satisfaction will plunge to an all-time low.
2. Socialization and growth during their thirties. Job and organizational satisfaction rise, reaching a peak in the late thirties or early forties.
3. A mid-career or mid-life crisis, starting in the middle to late thirties and ending in the mid-forties. Career choices and organizational commitment are once again questioned and adjustments made.
4. An increase in organizational satisfaction in their fifties, after accepting their life's choices and turning to the role of mentor to teach younger organizational members.
5. A decline in job satisfaction, beginning in the middle to late fifties, when employees begin a period of pre-retirement transition out of the work world. Their goal is to maintain career achievements rather than building new career goals.[4]

RESPECT FOR DIVERSITY AND CONFLICT RESOLUTION SKILLS

Managers of libraries in transition will need to have the ability to integrate people of different backgrounds into the organization by valuing their diversity and encouraging their different approaches to problem solving. Good managers will have developed respect for the intrinsic value of all human beings and strive to develop each person's abilities. Within a framework created by trust and respect, conflicts developing between people who work together can be used to develop the organization rather than letting them deteriorate into harmful personal attacks.

Research has proven that small groups accomplish more when dissenters are present than when everyone agrees with each other. The highest levels of creativity are found in organizations that encourage diversity and differences among people. Conflict can therefore be a valuable aid to spur creativity and productivity.

Managers in changing organizations must be skilled to depersonalize conflict and identify the underlying problem. They must respect and accept ideas expressed at all levels of the organization and examine them on their merits. When ideas become the property of an organization or group, divorced from the status of the individual who proposed them, they are more likely to be supported or used to generate more appropriate ideas for the problems at hand.

These managers must convince employees to support group decisions, even if they personally do not always agree. Employees must feel secure enough to express their reasons for disagreeing, even if the group chooses to disregard their reasoning. Consensus decisions have a high probability of being workable if they are supported by all. If the wrong decision is made or a crucial fact overlooked, group members are more likely to collectively accept the responsibility and try again. Those group members who disagree in principle to every decision made will eventually become ineffective, even if some of their points are valid.

Constructive conflict resolution can only occur in a climate of trust and positive thinking. Managers and employees must both feel ownership in the problems to be resolved. Selfish goals have to be sacrificed by all for the benefit of all. Managers will need to encourage people to speak out, state their objections, and support decisions made. If solutions are arrived at jointly, problems will be brought to the surface before they become serious.

Effective conflict resolution depends on adopting a "win-win" attitude and an integrative problem-solving approach. "Win-win" attitudes suggest that the people involved in a conflictive situation want to find a solution that is acceptable to all. This concept implies that the participants will benefit from mutual success, seek to establish the facts underlying a problem, accept conflicts as helpful, and look for a long-term solution rather than short-term gain.

To practice an integrative problem-solving approach, managers must accept the following beliefs while working with the problem:

1. A mutually acceptable solution to the problem is available;
2. A mutually acceptable solution to the problem is desirable;
3. Cooperation is a better approach to problem solving than competition;
4. Everyone is of equal value;
5. The opinions and desires of others are as legitimate as one's own opinions and desires;
6. Differences of opinion can be beneficial to a group, when handled constructively;
7. The other party or parties are trustworthy;
8. The other party will cooperate rather than compete.

After adopting the above attitudes, individuals or a group adopting an integrative problem-solving approach will define the problem together, define what constitutes a successful solution, generate possible alternative solutions, and select the best solution or the one least disagreeable to all.

In changing organizations the danger of "group think" should not be a major issue. Rather the opposite can be expected, since people will group themselves according to their willingness to embrace, oppose, or acquiesce to the changes. Should a "group think" mentality develop, however, which totally ignores or tolerates the opinions of other groups, outside experts can be engaged to challenge the views of managers or group members. They can question assumptions and values that group members are taking for granted. Their opinions may be given more credence, since they are removed from organizational pressures and hopefully are more objective.

ABILITY TO MOTIVATE

Motives can be defined as needs, wants, or drives of individuals. Motives are goal-directed. They can be conscious or subconscious. To successfully motivate subordinates, successful managers today must know the persons working for them well enough to determine their strongest needs. Motivation means finding the right incentives to help employees satisfy these needs while working within the inherent constraints of the organization.

Abraham Maslow developed a hierarchy of needs, based on their strengths during different stages of people's lives or careers. He suggests that human behavior is the result of our attempts to satisfy one or more of these needs. Each lower set of needs in the hierarchy must be at least partially satisfied before a person can search to satisfy those at the next higher level. Starting with the most basic and strongest needs, his hierarchy is as follows:

1. Physiological needs are those basic needs necessary to survive. They include food, shelter, and clothing.
2. Safety needs become predominant after physiological needs have been satisfied. They demand a measure of security and predictability, allowing some planning for the future.
3. Social needs, including friendship and acceptance by others, surface next. Persons with strong social needs will strive for meaningful relationships with others.
4. Esteem needs require respect and recognition from others and produce self-esteem and self-confidence based on expertise. People who are able to satisfy those needs feel that they are making a contribution and that they have an effect on their environment.
5. Self-actualization is the need to maximize one's potential; it seeks self-fulfillment and growth opportunities.[5]

Maslow believes that human behavior always seeks an equilibrium between the security and safety needs and those that foster growth and change. Because change is always threatening to the status quo, employees usually resist unless managers have the credibility to reassure them that their safety needs are not being endangered. People working in organizations today most likely are motivated to satisfy their higher order needs. They want gratifying social relationships, esteem for their contributions and expertise, and opportunities for self-actualization. Managers who think that satisfying physical and security needs is relieving them of their organizational obligations will likely have poor staff morale and low productivity.

Frederick Herzberg distinguishes between hygiene and motivation factors, which influence our behavior. Hygiene factors are such things as pay, fringe benefits, supervision, and the general working conditions. These factors do not motivate us positively because people take them for granted. If they are unacceptable, however, or below par they will make us feel unappreciated and unhappy with our jobs. Herzberg claims that people are motivated by a sense of responsibility, opportunities for development as workers and individuals, achievements, recognition, and chances for advancement.

Managers in transitional libraries may also want to use B. F. Skinner's insights on behavior modification. Skinner's theory suggests that managers who want to influence behavior need to create an environment where people are rewarded for behaving in desirable ways and punished or ignored for behaving inappropriately. Managers must determine what rewards inappropriate behavior brings for the employee. For example, temper tantrums may bring attention from coworkers; when the temper tantrum is ignored, the reward stops.

Providing positive feedback for work well done is still underutilized in today's organizations. Giving praise for specific achievements and positive behaviors reinforces the desirable actions at no cost.

Successful motivation then depends on how aware managers are of the needs and desires of their employees and whether they can give the rewards that will achieve the desired outcomes. Managers wishing to motivate employees in changing environments must clearly communicate what they consider to be acceptable work relationships. If employees fail to live up to expected responsibilities, managers must state how they view the situation. They need to suggest corrective actions and be specific about the negative consequences should no attempts be made to change. Criticism needs to be specific and detailed. It should include an offer to assist in working out the problems and developing a mutually acceptable plan to eliminate the issues under review.

More traditional approaches to motivation include:

- providing incentives for exceeding work standards
- creating a conditioning program where good work is consistently rewarded
- using the Scanlon plan, a forerunner of quality circles, where baselines for current productivity are established, departmental committees are formed to review and recommend suggestions for productivity improvements, and a steering committee is created to review, evaluate, and implement suggestions that have organizationwide implication
- establishing a "Management by Objectives" process in which mutual goals are set, management provides support for goal attainment, and individuals are responsible for the achievement of the goals
- using job enrichment to make positions more interesting

To successfully motivate today's employee, managers must be creative, innovative, and interested in each employee. They must communicate their concerns or their interests in each person's development and successes. They will know that good pay, working conditions, and fringe benefits are not enough to satisfy employees anymore. They are more interested in recognition, participation, and positive feedback for jobs well done.

Luther Middletown was director at the Circle Public Library. His staff was one of the best paid library staffs in the state and Luther never let them forget it.

Each time a legitimate library issue or problem needed to be discussed, Luther would say that he couldn't understand why they thought it was a problem. They were the highest paid staff in the state and they should be delighted to work at the Circle Public Library. When staff proposed to automate their serials records, Luther rejected the proposal. He claimed that the library did not have sufficient funds because such a large part of the library's budget went for staff salaries.

Luther Middletown's main motivation in life was money and he thought everybody else was similarly motivated. He could not understand why staff morale was so low, turnover so high, and people looked down whenever he reminded them of their high pay.

****

What else besides money motivates library staff? Do motivators stay constant over one's professional career?

ABILITY TO DELEGATE

Employees at all levels are ready and eager to make the decisions that affect their work and life. Managers in transitional organizations must be able to share the necessary information, resources, authority, and responsibility to enable subordinates to function in their expanded roles.

Delegation of decision making and authority does not just happen; it must be planned for, with expectations clarified and performance standards agreed upon. The goals to be achieved have to be defined by management or negotiated between employee and manager. Staff must be able to make the necessary decisions or be developed to accept the responsibility inherent in participation.

Managers of changing organizations often walk a fine line between leaving subordinates alone to perform their work without interference and instituting a monitoring system that lets the managers know when the organizational goals are at risk because of inadequate decision making. During transition a lot of attention will have to be paid appropriately to training people to take on additional responsibilities and to allow them the opportunity to make mistakes without abandoning the efforts toward sharing responsibilities. The new managers will not look at power as something to be enjoyed for its own sake but as something to be shared to achieve the common good. They will not take credit for something they accomplished but will pride themselves on how well their subordinates are taking on additional responsibilities to help improve overall organizational effectiveness. They will succeed because of the cooperation and ability of their subordinates, not because they think their own skills are superior.

Increased delegation will free managers to concentrate on planning and goal setting, while letting subordinates grow and develop to become greater assets to the organization.

Effective delegation is a skill that has to be acquired. The most frequently made mistakes in delegating include:

- retaining too much control over the process
- not providing the necessary resources to accomplish a task
- not providing the employee with the relevant information that affects his or her assignment

- expressing only criticism with the efforts of employees
- not delegating at all because the subordinate does not yet possess all the required skills necessary to complete the assignment

Delegation is based on the division of labor concept. Managers are hired to organize people and motivate them to perform the work necessary for the achievement of company goals. It is not necessary or desirable for managers to do the work themselves just because they think they can do it better.

Effective managers always ask themselves if a particular work assignment can be delegated. If the answer is yes, they will:

1. Communicate the specific results they hope to achieve
2. Monitor a subordinate's progress and provide assistance, when necessary
3. Clarify expectations and goals as needed
4. Provide positive feedback to subordinates
5. Be fair in their assessment of the goals achieved
6. Provide encouragement to subordinates and themselves to try again, if the first attempts at delegation do not achieve exactly the desired outcomes

---

Sonja Archer was the successful candidate for the new position of Community Outreach librarian at the Hillside Public Library. She had been on the staff of the library for about 10 years and had worked on the committee that set up the guidelines to establish a community outreach program. Sonja was very pleased about her new job and eagerly waited to have a conference with her supervisor, Mark Deadrick, to discuss her responsibilities and how to proceed.

Mark was very much involved with rearranging the library's reading room and assumed that Sonja, since she worked on the guidelines committee, would have a good idea how to get started. Sonja continued to perform the responsibilities she had in her old job because nobody had been hired yet to replace her. Her former colleagues were happy that she was still helping out. However, the overburdened Sonja became increasingly anxious and irritable.

After the move was completed three months later, Mark finally set up a meeting with Sonja to discuss the proposal and the preliminary goals he assumed she had developed since she took over her new responsibilities. The meeting went badly. Sonja was in tears and wanted to resign, while Mark was angry at her lack of leadership and initiative. They decided to meet again in two days to discuss what went wrong and make some decisions on how to proceed.

****

Was Mark a good delegator? What assumptions can we make about the organizational climate at Hillside Public and why? What steps could Sonja have taken?

Developing and training subordinates are important parts of the delegating process. Managers must offer opportunities for employees to take on additional responsibilities, and if a subordinate wants to progress, the necessary skills for the tasks must be taught. Providing very specific guidelines, goals, and time frames, and scheduling feedback sessions are very important as the delegating process begins. It involves risk taking and trust on the part of both parties, who must be willing to ask questions if instructions appear nonexistent or are unclear, and provide constructive feedback if progress is not as expected. Subordinates will feel very insecure and tentative about their new assignments and will need frequent interactions and reassurances. As their self-confidence and willingness to take on more projects increase so will the manager's trust and ability to delegate. As a result a participative organization will evolve, which uses the talents of all employees.

An open and supportive organizational climate is essential for effective delegation to occur at all levels of the organization. If a library does not have the trust and commitment of employees, good communication, and clear goals, delegation will not be successful. If managers themselves are confused about their own responsibilities and are not knowledgeable about the organizational mission and goals, they will be inadequate delegators because they will not be able to communicate the importance of the responsibilities delegated.

Delegation increases as managers move up in an organizational hierarchy. A rule of thumb is that a lower-level supervisor may delegate about 25 percent of his or her work, while a middle manager needs to delegate about 50 percent; a top executive, in turn, may delegate up to 95 percent of his or her work load.

There are, however, tasks that can never be delegated. They include incomplete assignments, personal projects, personnel problems in your area of responsibility, and establishing effective work relationships with colleagues and peers.

ABILITY TO MAKE DECISIONS

In changing organizations effective managers need to be able to make decisions based on limited facts and without knowing all the possible alternatives. They must possess an ability to think on their feet, have good judgment, and generally anticipate the consequences of their decisions. If managers are unable to accept the risk of making decisions based on limited information, they will postpone making a decision, with often worse consequences than making a wrong decision. Decision making is a never-ending requirement of all managerial positions. Decisions or refusals to make decisions create chain reactions which in turn demand decisions again.

The most difficult decisions often involve disciplinary actions. Managers tend to avoid making them because they like to think that the infraction or problem was a one-time occurrence and will not happen again. Many believe that the employee knows better and therefore will not repeat the inappropriate behavior and action. They have difficulties in understanding why somebody acts in a self-defeating, immature, or ethically wrong way and they wait until the problem becomes so obvious that it affects the morale and work of an entire department or division. Then they become angry at being forced to do something, and the reprimand or punishment is out of proportion to the infraction committed.

Making disciplinary decisions is an important managerial responsibility in changing organizations. Such decisions need to be used to communicate new expectations and a willingness for the manager to help the employee fulfill those expectations. If made in a timely manner, they will extinguish undesirable behavior before it becomes an accepted pattern that will be difficult to change. Managers need to remember that they are not the cause of having to make the decision. The employee who is either ignorant of expectations or is unwilling to change is creating the need for intervention. Employees need to accept responsibilities for their actions just as the manager needs to act on his or her responsibility to address problems.

There are situations where decisions need to be postponed or involve other people. They include those situations where other employees or departments are significantly affected by the decisions to be made and where the consequences of decisions can be very costly.

Herbert A. Simon identified two decision-making models in his classic management book *Administrative Behavior: A Study of Decision-Making Processes in Administrative Organizations.* The maximizing process entails:

- Careful and precisely defined decision criteria
- An awareness of all possible alternatives
- An awareness of all possible results of each alternative
- An evaluation of the results of each alternative against the decision criteria
- A ranking of the alternatives from most desirable to least desirable based on the decision criteria
- A selection of the alternatives that rank the highest based on the decision criteria. [6]

It is obvious that managers in transitional organizations will rarely, if ever, have the time and luxury to use all the steps outlined above. Instead they are most likely to use the satisficing decision-making model which involves the following:

- An awareness of only a limited number of decision criteria
- An awareness of only a limited number of alternatives
- An examination of only a few of the consequences of each alternative
- A ranking of a limited number of alternatives based on the decision criteria
- A selection of the most satisfactory or least undesirable alternative based on the limited number of decision criteria[7]

Libraries moving toward participative environments will include as many people as possible in the decision-making process. Decisions are made in response to perceived problems that need to be remedied. For good decision making to occur it is essential that employees believe that a problem actually exists that demands a decision. Involvement in the problem definition is therefore the first essential step toward joint decision making. Those employees who will not perceive a problem will most likely prefer the status quo and not be motivated enough to seek solutions.

Frances O'Connor was retiring after 30 years with Southern Regional University. For the last 15 years she held the position of Head of Acquisitions. She was a good supervisor and most of the people working for her had been in the department for almost as long as Frances. Most had carved out their own area of responsibility and did their work with minimum supervision.

A national search was conducted for Frances's successor and the library was very fortunate to hire Liza Barnes, who had been Assistant Head of Acquisitions at a major university library. She came highly recommended by supervisors, colleagues, and peers. Liza had the reputation of a go-getter and was very active in the profession. She was anxious to finally manage her own department and solidify her reputation in the acquisitions field.

From the first day Liza asked questions of her staff about procedures, policies, work assignments, and staffing levels. In her second staff meeting, Liza announced that she planned to make a number of changes to bring the library in line with what other acquisitions departments had done years ago. She handed each person their new work assignments in writing, describing all the new procedures in detail, and told them to start implementing the changes by the following Monday.

She tried to tell the staff how confident she was in their ability and how excited she was to really make their work more efficient, but a deadly silence had fallen over the conference room and nobody even looked in her direction. Everybody appeared busy reading their instructions. Liza told them she would be available for their questions and wished them all much success in their new jobs.

****

What do you think will happen next? Is Liza wrong in making changes to run the department more efficiently? How would you have handled the situation?

Most people prefer the familiar, especially if they had a part in creating their own work environment and procedures. To bring about change in such situations, the employees themselves need to be educated first about other, more productive, ways of doing a particular work assignment. Encouraging employees to visit other libraries, reading professional literature, and attending conferences and workshops may be the first steps toward heightening their awareness that their way of performing their responsibilities needs to be changed. They can become advocates of change for their coworkers by reporting back how things can be done much better and building positive expectations in the work group. Making decisions in organizations and about one's work is a privilege and a responsibility that must be cherished and used with care.

COMMITMENT TO TEAM MANAGEMENT

The ability to commit groups of people toward the accomplishment of common goals is an essential requirement for managers. Establishing a climate for team management and developing effective teams will facilitate organizational change because a large number of employees will be actively involved in assessing the organizational problems and implementing solutions and strategies they developed.

Research has shown that decisions made by groups of people are more accurate, albeit slower, than those made by most individuals. Superior individuals, however, make better decisions than groups and do so with more accuracy, speed, and efficiency.

In transitional libraries, team management efforts are not only advisable for good decision making but desirable as a developmental tool for employees. Such efforts will teach a large number of subordinates the constraints under which decisions have to be made and the difficulties in analyzing problems correctly. In addition, team management fosters the acceptance of change, which is often more crucial than the speed with which decisions have to be made. Because transitional libraries increase in complexity, the team approach to management increases communication, expertise, decision-making ability, and commitment to the change process throughout the organization. The time and effort spent to develop effective teams is therefore a worthwhile investment and will bring many unplanned for but desirable benefits.

Teams are distinguishable from other work groups because:

- a high level of communication exists among their members
- personal relationships are formed

- 'I, me, mine' are replaced by 'we, us, and ours'
- a low level of jealousy promotes cooperation
- a high level of trust exists among team members
- similarities and differences among team members are utilized
- members have the feeling that they are part of everything that goes on within the team[8]

Teams increase employees' sense of belonging and give them some sense of stability and certainty when everything else in the organization appears to be in a state of flux. Teams maintain their own equilibrium and do not require as much manager intervention as do individuals. At their best, teams will resolve their own conflicts, train their own members, evaluate their own performance, and discipline team members if necessary. This frees management's energy to pursue and explore other issues and plan for the future.

Not all employees are suited to work in teams; over- or under-achievers usually reject the concept of team management or are rejected by team members for the obvious reasons. Effective team members need to be interested in the welfare and achievement of others. They should have an encouraging, nurturing attitude; be flexible, friendly; have the needed skills; and have enough self-confidence to speak up and not be intimidated by other team members.

Team members depend on each other for success, support, emotional well-being, training, and recognition. Building teams therefore takes time since relationships must develop and trust must be fostered between members. Vern Goldsmith uses the following illustration to show how trust/relationships form:

TRUST/RELATIONSHIP MODEL

Exchange of basic information
Exchange of basic ideas
Exchange of feelings
Trust
Open Communication
Commitment to the Relationship
Dependence
Independence
Interdependence[9]

Team members have to learn to be open with each other, to share ideas, feelings, common goals, and problems. They come to know as much about each other's likes and dislikes at work as outside of work. They understand each other's motivations, strengths, and weaknesses and combine their efforts for the success of their team. They build organizational cohesiveness based on common goals and interests. The skills gained in team work can later be used to address greater organizational concerns and issues.

NETWORKING

Managers of changing libraries need to be in touch with other libraries in order to exchange ideas, ask for constructive criticism, and learn from the mistakes of others. Networking among libraries that undergo similar changes can provide:

- encouragement to persist despite setbacks
- expertise that may not be found in one's own organization
- constructive criticism on planned actions
- advice on how to avoid common pitfalls experienced by others
- an avenue to share one's successes for the advancement of the profession

Networking can provide a much needed support group when managers experience problems or difficulties in their change efforts. Networking will put problems in proper perspective and provide comfort, if needed, because no organization is without its problems. Reading about other organizations' experiences or hearing a colleague describe an attempted program that failed will provide insights and new ideas. Just knowing that one's own library is actually addressing problems will give many managers the strength to continue dealing with the many unanticipated minor irritations that inevitably accompany all changes.

Luckily there are usually libraries that are ahead of one's own organizational efforts just as there are always those who are far behind. Networking lets you learn from those ahead and gain comfort from those behind. It feels gratifying to share your own experiences with an eager colleague and it gives you renewed resolve to continue the everlasting struggle to improve libraries for the benefit of their patrons and the people who have to do the work. Networking lets you know there is hope for success, generally, and need for the expertise you are developing in your present situation, specifically.

MENTORING

Like networking, mentoring instills in colleagues and subordinates the excitement for change and growth and contributes to the overall advancement of the profession. Opportunities, successes, and pitfalls can be shared to prevent others from having to reinvent the wheel or make the same mistakes.

Mentoring often provides a better teaching and learning experience than course work and books. It is based on experience, and if the experience has been effective, mentoring will help other professionals develop. Mentoring allows the mentor to develop a connectedness with the future of one's chosen profession and a sense of pride in giving one's best to a colleague.

All librarians should function as mentors to others who are moving into and upward within the profession. They will find that through mentoring, as through other forms of teaching, the teacher usually gains more than the pupil by having the satisfaction of seeing the person mentored grow, gain in expertise and confidence, and make a contribution to the profession. Mentoring should happen at all levels of the organization and is not limited to one's subordinates. Peers and colleagues are equally receptive and grateful to be taken under an expert's wing, learning aspects of librarianship to which they were previously not exposed. Although those mentored hopefully outgrow the need for that special relationship, if the mentoring is successful, they will usually become good friends who still value each other's advice on career goals and work problems.

WOMEN MANAGERS

Women managers will play an important role in libraries in transition because they will, to a large degree, represent the values, hopes, and ambitions of the majority of library workers who are female. They will reemphasize the goals of cooperation, team work, and empathy, and foster the development of all human resources. By providing a different outlook on problems, the solutions themselves will become better if women managers' organizations are open and willing to incorporate their influence. Women managers, grounded in the reality of work through years of experience at lower levels, will help balance the ideal with the possible. Relying on their dedication to the profession, creativity, and concern for others, organizational dynamics will change. Women managers' willingness to verbalize issues should facilitate organizational communication, and issues can be addressed sooner, once they are out in the open.

Women managers will, however, also experience skepticism about their abilities, accusations of inexperience, and emotional instability, and manipulative power plays. The behavior patterns that may be acceptable in a man may not be tolerated in a woman.

Because managerial opportunities have been denied to them for so long, women will place greater emphasis on continuing education, encourage others to develop their abilities, and help each other to overcome weaknesses. Women need to learn to see the overall picture and free themselves from being too closely involved in the day-to-day activities they supervise. Although they may still feel they can do the jobs they left behind better than anyone else, those jobs are somebody else's responsibility now; the person who succeeded them needs time and opportunity to learn and grow.

In order to have progressed to the managerial ranks, women generally have had to be flexible, assertive, knowledgeable, cooperative, and self-directed, all qualities needed in effective organizations. Women managers will become a primary force in changing library organizations by balancing and enriching the traditional management team and by challenging old assumptions. It is inconceivable to envision a library in transition without a number of women managers.

NOTES

1. Richard L. Schott, "The Psychological Developments of Adults: Implications for Public Administration." *Public Administration Review* 46 (November/December 1986): 665–66.

2. Schott, p. 666.

3. Michael Maccoby, *The Leader*. New York: Simon & Schuster, 1981, p. 49.

4. Manfred Kets de Vries, et al, "Using the Life Cycle to Anticipate Satisfaction at Work." *Journal of Forecasting* 3 (1984): 164.

5. Paul Hersey and Kenneth H. Blanchard, *Management of Organizational Behavior: Utilizing Human Resources*. 3d ed. Englewood Cliffs, NJ: Prentice Hall, 1977, pp. 30-34.

6. Joseph F. Byrnes created this list, based on the work of Herbert A. Simon. Byrnes' list appears in *How to Make Better Decisions. Workbook*. New York: American Management Associations Extension Institute, 1982, p. 19.

7. Joseph F. Byrnes created this list, based on the work of Herbert A. Simon. Byrnes' list appears in *How to Make Better Decisions. Workbook*. New York: American Management Associations Extension Institute, 1982, p. 20.

8. Vern Goldsmith, *Effective Team Building. Workbook*. New York: American Management Associations Extension Institute, 1980, p. 13.

9. Goldsmith, p. 49.

Chapter 6
Managerial Tools for Changing Organizational Roles

During the last decade a proliferation of management books has created an awareness of and an interest in new managerial tools designed to increase productivity and humanize the workplace. Global competition in all areas requires constant innovation. Managers everywhere are looking for new ways to increase employee commitment, creativity, and participation. As the focus on short-term profits is replaced by a commitment to long-term problem solving, organizations are able to invest in the oftentimes consuming task of involving employees in the decision-making processes to generate better ideas to ensure their viability.

This chapter will outline and discuss some of the common managerial tools that will be helpful for managing libraries in transition.

BUILDING SELF-CONFIDENCE IN EMPLOYEES

Changing organizations need competent employees with clear values, a sense of personal security, and knowledge of who they are (because stability, purpose, and direction in their lives cannot be provided by the organization but must come from within).

Values and confidence do not miraculously appear in people's lives. They are acquired through making false starts, surviving crises, knowing oneself, determining one's role in society, developing as a human being. Effective people have learned to cope with situational pressures, knowing that crises present challenges to test them and their skills.

To increase employees' self-confidence, managers have to start with building their self-esteem. Self-esteem is the evaluation we make of ourselves. It is continually changing and evolving. It is based on our beliefs about our competence in the roles we choose to play. This belief is strongly influenced by the way people have interacted with us in the past and what we perceive to be expected of us in the present. To change someone's self-confidence, a manager must change that person's view of him or herself. This is accomplished by changing the interaction patterns between the employee and the managers. If the interaction patterns remain the same, employees will remain unmotivated to change.

All of our past interaction patterns become a part of us. We catalog them and call upon them in new situations if we think that they will work for us. The changes that occur in us during the course of our careers are changes in the nature of our constructed selves. Psychology has proven that we can develop new attitudes and values, adopt new images of ourselves, acquire new competencies, and create new ways of thinking, feeling, and behaving.

A high correlation exists between developing a higher self-esteem and improved job performance. Organizational development efforts, for example, prove successful when changes in self-esteem occur. Abraham Korman of the University of Michigan provides evidence that people attempt to behave in a manner consistent with their own self-image, that if employees see themselves as failures on the job, they will not put forth much effort, their performance will be poor, and a self-fulfilling cycle will be set in motion. Consequently the most successful managerial strategy to improve performance will focus on enhancing employees' self-image. If management establishes high performance expectations, employees will try to live up to those expectations.

Self-insight on the part of the employees is a prerequisite for improvement of skills. One must become aware of inadequacies or opportunities before being interested in developing skills. Managers themselves must develop their own self-esteem as well as that of others. If we understand the kind of person we are in general, our roots, and where we are headed, we will present ourselves as capable and competent. Others will pick up on this self-confidence and it will become reinforcing. Self-esteem is neither arrogance nor ignorance. It is an evaluation that we all make and customarily maintain of ourselves. It expresses our belief in our capabilities.

Self-esteem and self-confidence are highly dependent on the degree to which people's successes approach their expectations in those areas that are important to them. Although self-esteem reflects the self-evaluation people make of themselves, this evaluation is in turn heavily dependent on the evaluation that they believe other "important" people are making of them.

People with low self-esteem tend to be suspicious of other people. They believe that others are trying to "get them" in some way or to work some kind of angle. They don't like themselves very much and other people tend to regard them similarly. People with low self-esteem tend to view any critique as negative criticism and see it as a confirmation of their inadequacies. Self-confident people view criticism as a natural outgrowth of the essential task of assessing and evaluating performance.

Managers who feel confident in most social interactions and who have a high sense of personal worth are successful because they are able to act quickly and decisively in pressured situations. Since management is characterized by an almost innumerable amount of activities that require quick action and ad hoc wisdom, people who are not plagued by self-doubt or disillusionment are naturally going to better handle the demands of the job.

The view we have of ourselves is learned; it is not inherited and it is not static. A major study of the lives of 200 men over a period of 40 years at Harvard found that for the men in the study, the circumstances of their upbringing or occupation had less to do with successful coping than how each one defined his ability to meet challenges head on and do whatever was necessary to come out on top. Requirements for coping well with one's world seemed to include altruism, humor, suppression of discomfort, anticipation, hopefulness, and a forward-looking attitude.

The process by which these men learned to cope successfully included a sequential mastering of one's body, reality, and emotions. The process emphasizes that one learns most about one's self through association with others. People become more aware of who they are not from introspection but from interaction.[1]

What can managers or employees do to increase their own self-confidence? One step is to choose a model one wants to emulate. Consciously identifying and selecting a model and noticing what that person does and how he or she approaches and resolves tasks can increase one's own personal effectiveness, provided, of course, that one selects a good model. Observing and recording how a person approaches tasks is important.

Learning the way we communicate with others can be very important. We need to observe how other people react to the things we say or do. Spending the time observing the consequences we produce in others can be extremely useful. The people we work with can also be good sources of feedback on how we communicate.

In order to motivate people to give their best on the job, managerial expectations about job skills must be very high. Many people provide too low job expectations for employees. Once high expectations are communicated, employees need to receive continuous feedback about their performance; appraisal of one's achievement by others is important to reinforce the newly developing self-image of employees. New organizational efforts in this area include weight reduction, wellness and fitness programs, to name but two avenues for creating a better self-image among employees.

CONTINUING EDUCATION AND STAFF TRAINING

Continuing education and training seminars offered by libraries, professional organizations, and private vendors are proliferating. Attendance and participation continue to grow despite financial constraints of libraries, attesting to the importance of and need for such activities. Programs focus on technical competencies, human resource management skills, and assistance in human development efforts. Their offers range from training for basic job-specific skills to broader managerial topics like adapting to organizational change, risk-taking, and managing conflict.

Libraries in transition have special needs concerning staff development and training, since both have to be directed toward understanding and dealing with moving targets. Although the organization may have a general idea or plan toward which it wants to develop, many of the changes create unforeseen consequences; constant readjustments are necessary in goals and day-to-day activities. Continuing education and staff development activities, therefore, should encompass both training for specific skills and creating an understanding of the special requirements imposed by changing organizations. Fortunately, in this case, most libraries, like other bureaucratic non-profit organizations, are usually not on the cutting edge of organizational development but are able to learn from the experiences in the private sector. The few libraries willing and able to experiment with new programs, approaches to management, and new organizational structures do it mostly because of financial constraints. They will be observed and analyzed carefully for years before others will jump on the bandwagon.

By the time change becomes inevitable within the majority of libraries, a substantial body of literature in and outside the field will exist to facilitate the change efforts of the other libraries. Change can then be put into its proper perspective as a fact of life that institutions and individuals undergo constantly. The argument that planning for change is better than having it forced on you by circumstances (mostly in the form of budget cuts) will make more sense.

Libraries in transition that want to consciously manage their change efforts need to help their staff understand the change process and how they can positively participate. Creating an overall framework that shows that the considered changes are a natural evolution from current practices, assessing that the organization has the expertise and climate to implement proposed changes, and providing seminars to teach the specific skills still thought to be lacking may be the necessary initial staff development programs that support the planning stage for a major organizational change effort. Management experts, colleagues from libraries that have already undergone similar changes, or staff members interested in organizational development can be engaged to share their knowledge and perspective and provide the organization with the concepts and techniques necessary to discuss and plan for changes.

An inventory of techniques already used in a particular institution will be helpful to convey the message that everybody already has some of the skills necessary to move toward a new organization. Personal and organizational action plans can be developed to set goals for practicing and internalizing new techniques and providing evaluation timeframes to monitor success or failure of goals attainment.

Simultaneously with the acquisition of intellectual knowledge of change and its nature, libraries may want to provide stress management seminars, health improvement activities, and other support mechanisms to enable employees to cope with the additional psychological and physical demands imposed by changes. Those employees who are unable or unwilling to accept the inevitability of change can be provided with career counseling, outplacement services, or reassignment to more structured positions if possible.

Feedback sessions in which the entire organization participates, together with opportunities for individuals to share their perceptions with managers and fellow employees, should be scheduled at regular intervals to assess problems, successes, and the general state of the organization. Care should be taken to listen to divergent viewpoints and address shared problems. Feedback will stop if employees feel that negative feedback, when justified, is ignored; problems will fester until they become major issues. Expressing appreciation for negative feedback will sometimes ensure the success of a program, because employees will be willing to help work out the problems if they perceive that their opinions count and are valued.

Libraries committed to the value of continuing education and staff development may want to develop a policy explaining:

- the purpose and goals of a staff development program
- the types of activities included and offered
- the responsibilities of the organization and certain staff members for providing continuing education activities
- the resources allocated to staff development in terms of educational time off and travel funds
- the responsibilities of the employees to participate for their own growth and development
- the consideration given participation in staff development activities as part of the overall performance evaluation
- the process of scheduling staff development activities
- the selection process for attending programs, if participation is limited or travel is necessary
- the evaluation process for programs
- the record keeping system for staff attendance

Relevant continuing education and training programs are based on staff development needs assessments performed at least annually. A sample needs assessment that you may want to use appears on page 92. Needs assessments will confirm that supervisory and human relation skills seminars remain a major concern. It is advisable to offer at least one or two basic supervisory skills seminars each year to reinforce the organizational commitment to good supervisory practices and reinforce its managerial philosophy with new managers. Specific skills like motivation, delegation, listening, evaluations, disciplinary actions, hiring, training and interviewing, for example, can be acquired or refined through a multitude of excellent audio-visual programs, which supervisors can use as needed.

Figure 1. Staff Development Needs Assessment

Please take a few minutes to fill out the following questionnaire. Your answers will assist me in developing an appropriate staff development program for the coming year.

1. Do you have supervisory responsibilities?
   yes _____ no _____
2. How long have you been employed at the Library?
   years _____ months _____
3. Position Classification or Title:
   _____

4. Which times of the week are best for you to attend staff development activities? Please indicate the three best time periods: _____
   _____

5. Please mark which of the following staff development topics would be of help to you during the coming year:

Topics:	Not helpful	Somewhat helpful	Very Helpful
Affirmative Action			
Automated Systems			
Collection Development			
Communication Skills			
Conflict Resolution			
Database Searching			
Delegation			
Disciplinary Actions			
Evaluations			
Feedback Skills			
Grant Writing			
Interpersonal Relations			
Interviewing			
Motivation			
Negotiations			
Organizational Development			
Participative Management			
PCs and Software			
Planning			
Presentation Skills			
Preservation			
Problem Solving			
Recruiting			
Stress Management			
Team Building			
Time Management			
Writing Skills			
Other			

Rank *six* of the topics you marked *very helpful* as your priorities for developmental activities this year: _____
_____

Thanks.

[Return this questionnaire to the Library Personnel Office.]

While there are some developmental needs common to all library employees, others are more group- or department-specific or are of interest to only a small number of individuals. Special programs, most of them task-oriented, may be designed to focus on departmental needs. Experts within the group or library are usually called on to conduct such sessions after they receive training through professional organizations, vendors, other libraries, or formal course work.

Many libraries, especially those with faculty status for professional staff, provide opportunities for individual staff members to conduct in-depth research activities, pursue degree programs, or request study leaves for lengthy periods. Approval of these activities is usually dependent on their purpose and usefulness to the institution and/or profession. Applications may have to be approved by authorities outside the library, depending on the type of leave requested.

Responsibilities for staff development activities are most often assigned to a Personnel Librarian and/or staff development committee. More recently a few ARL libraries have established positions which are solely responsible for staff development programs. The involvement of committees in determining staff development needs and planning programs ensures staff input and accountability for the relevance of programs.

INTERNSHIPS

Developing training programs and internships for particular groups already employed within a changing library can be used to motivate individuals and groups to acquire new skills and enhance productivity and efficiency. Librarians who have functionally plateaued in their area of expertise may be revitalized through working in several different departments. Training programs developed for such purposes should take into consideration the trainee's expertise and show the interrelationship between the librarian's regular responsibilities and how they can be applied in the training areas. If a team approach to management is developed, supervisory responsibilities may be shared among several team members who previously had no line responsibilities. Such an arrangement may create an awareness of the difficulties and complexities of supervision but also identify desired competencies which may lead to a rethinking of long term career goals.

Employees who have plateaued or are at the top of the career ladder within an institution can remain interested and contributing members of the organization if they are willing to broaden their skills and be open to new training opportunities. The profession is changing so rapidly that limitations on skills development are self-imposed and ultimately self-defeating. Managers in transition have the difficult task of making their staffs aware of this fact and providing them with the necessary opportunities to overcome inertia and self-satisfaction.

Training and internship programs can also develop promotional opportunities for support staff in lower classifications. Because their job responsibilities are often narrowly defined, their knowledge of other library departments and functions is often very limited. Working in other departments for a specified length of time will increase specific skills necessary for promotion into upward classifications when vacancies occur. It will also benefit the library by developing employee training skills. An example of an affirmative action training/internship program is included in the appendix.

MEETINGS

Effective use of all types of meetings is another device used in organizations to facilitate changes. Meetings fall into two general categories: meetings that are sustaining in nature and are used for communication, information, or morale building purposes, and meetings that are goal- or task-oriented. Sustaining meetings include staff and advisory group meetings, while goal- or task-oriented meetings consist of production or program meetings, committee meetings, and task forces.

Staff meetings are sustaining. They are held within departments or divisions to relate policies or new procedures, disseminate information, or discuss problems. They should be held periodically to ensure that everyone is being kept informed or to address problems that are affecting morale. To serve its purpose, the meeting must be conducted properly. Usually an announced agenda is preferred but there are occasions when creating an agenda within the context of the meetings is effective in bringing problems to the surface.

Staff meetings of the entire organization are also a useful device to relate organizationwide policies and to keep staff abreast of the "state of the library."

Advisory group meetings, such as meetings of key managers, are another type of sustaining meeting. These are effective in disseminating information to the organization as a whole through the use of the hierarchy.

Staff groups that participate in sustaining meetings can also be used for *goal-* or *task-oriented meetings*. Staff or advisory groups can be formed to discuss ways to resolve specific and limited problems or to generate new ideas. It is usually more effective to use smaller groups to resolve problems or generate ideas. In a *production* or *program meeting* employees come together to discuss a common project, design a specific procedure, or resolve workflow issues involving just that group.

Committee meetings are another type of goal- or task-oriented meeting. Committees are formed when input for major decisions is needed. Committee membership is drawn from the different areas that are affected by the problem to be resolved or policy or procedure to be designed. A committee should be composed of people with different insights and viewpoints concerning the common issue. Committees are specifically created for problem solving or policy design. Committee meetings are examples of decision making implemented in a democratic manner through use of the advisory or consultative process.

Task forces can be defined as ad hoc committees, formed to resolve one particular and narrowly defined problem. Task force charges should be well defined and limited to find the solution for one issue. It is understood that the group of individuals working on a task will disband after a solution is found. A task force usually consists of people who are affected by the problem to be resolved; membership cuts across organizational and hierarchical lines.

In transitional organizations the use of task forces is often more acceptable than the creation of standing committees. Employees who have little experience in participative decision making will feel more productive working on a specific problem than being involved in many standing committees whose purposes are not always clear. Employees in changing environments sometimes will feel "overburdened" by the demands of participation. They perceive all those meetings as "added" responsibilities, and like most employees, they probably already feel overworked. Task forces have a definite ending date. Task forces are therefore a good bridging strategy to foster participation and build cooperation in the organization.

Since task forces need to involve those employees who are affected by the problem, regardless of their status or rank, they tend to break down hierarchical structures and build respect for the expertise of members. Task forces are excellent for planning inventories and moves, developing signage systems, creating manuals, and working out schedules.

There are some general guidelines applicable to all productive meetings. When calling a meeting, the objective of the meeting should be stated with an agenda distributed, if there is one. The timing of a meeting is also important. When should meetings be held?

- When there is adequate preparation time
- When feedback is needed
- When several people need to be involved
- When interaction is necessary to promote creativity or for group analysis of a situation
- When information must be acted upon
- When a controversy must be addressed

A meeting should *not* be called if:

- There is inadequate preparation time
- Communication is to be one way and no feedback is to be allowed
- A problem can be resolved easily without involvement of several people
- Input is not needed
- Conflict is not likely

Often committees have not been used effectively within libraries. They sometimes are used to rubber stamp a decision that has already been made or they are treated as conduits to higher management. At other times the scope of committee power and responsibilities is not clearly defined. Committees should not be forced to function under pressure. Members of committees should be given credit for their work. Everyone should have responsibility for specific parts of the task. Everyone should be treated equally when serving on committees. Professional staff should not receive preferential treatment nor should their opinions be regarded as more valuable than those of support staff. Time frames should be kept reasonable. Membership on committees should have a definite term of service. The existence of the committees themselves should have a deadline at which time the committees will cease to exist or there will be some review of their reason for existence.

Management theory suggests that, when creating committees, selecting an odd number of members is preferable since even-numbered groups experience more disagreements, generate fewer suggestions, and have more problems with decisions. Generally goal-oriented groups such as committees should be as small in size as possible; a membership of five or seven appears most productive.

In any type of meeting, the person in charge should serve as a mediator, being supportive of the process but attempting to expedite the meeting. The leader should state the problem or objective, directing clarification of the issues surrounding it. He or she should elicit identification of several alternative solutions, keeping the discussion directed toward resolving the objective of the meeting, and helping the group arrive at a consensus decision. If there are hidden agendas, they should be identified and discussed. The meeting leader is also responsible for identifying and directing different personnel problems that may arise from participants who are dominating, negative, quiet, or who evidence other hindering attributes.

TECHNIQUES TO USE IN MEETINGS

There are several effective techniques that can be used to make meetings more productive.

Idea Exchanges/Brainstorming Sessions

To encourage the creative process, meetings can be used as a platform for the exchange of ideas, or as brainstorming sessions. While the objective of an idea exchange should be made known, a rigid agenda should not be prepared in advance. Instead, participants should be apprised of the objective of the session, the time frame, and general meeting guidelines:

- Allow some "think time" at the beginning of the meeting
- All ideas are valid
- All ideas will be recorded
- Everyone contributes
- Ideas will not be evaluated

After the idea exchange, the list of ideas should be distributed and the group then can narrow the list to the ones potentially implementable.

Brainstorming works similarly. It is a procedure wherein members are encouraged to generate alternative suggestions in a completely non-evaluative group atmosphere. For example, a manager might ask, "What are some ways that we might use to decrease our backlog of interlibrary loan requests?" Group members would then offer alternative solutions aloud to the group. All group members are encouraged to offer solutions, no matter how unusual they may seem. One member of the group is assigned the responsibility of recording all the suggestions. No group member is allowed to make evaluative statements during the brainstorming session. The ideas are then evaluated in later sessions.

Nominal Group Technique

Nominal group technique takes advantage of the fact that some people are able to generate more ideas working separately than in a group. In this procedure, group members write down ideas or solutions to a problem, but they do it privately on slips of paper. No discussion is allowed at this point. In the next phase of the procedure, each group member is asked to contribute one of his or her ideas. These ideas are then written on a flipchart or chalkboard. No evaluation of ideas is permitted at this point. Later in this phase, group members may "pass" if they are out of ideas or may offer new ideas not on their original lists. Group members are encouraged to build on others' ideas. After all ideas are posed, questions may be asked for clarification. Again, no evaluation is allowed until after all ideas are posted and understood by everyone.

Synectics Techniques

These techniques use fantasy and analogy to facilitate creativity and new perspectives on old problems. The goal is to attempt to redefine long-standing group problems in such a way that a solution becomes possible. To begin this procedure, the leader describes a problem. The problem is explained in depth by knowledgeable members of the group. All members are then asked to write one or more restatements of the problem, as they see it. In these restatements, members are encouraged to use fantasy and to think in terms of wishful goals, no matter how unrealistic they may seem. In the next phase, the leader chooses one of the restatements for the group to focus on. No attempt is made to reach consensus on the definition of the problem at this point. Rather, honest expression and understanding of group members' ideas is stressed. In one of the more straightforward techniques, the next step is for members to think of analogies to the restated problem in other settings in the hopes that strategies that have proven effective in other settings might be applied in the current situation.

Risk

This procedure focuses on an assessment of the risks of possible negative consequences that might occur as a result of the implementation of a chosen solution to a problem. To begin the procedure, group members privately list all the possible negative consequences that they feel might result from the implementation of a chosen problem solution. In the next phase of *Risk*, these ideas are listed on a flipchart or chalkboard. This listing is done in a nonevaluative group atmosphere. Next, group members are asked to rank each of the negative consequences in terms of the possibility of its being realized. After the negative consequences have been ranked in this manner, the top "risks" are selected for further discussion. The final step in this process is for the group to design contingency plans in the event that the "risks" become reality. In this way, the group is prepared for several scenarios that may take place.

COMMUNICATION CHANNELS

Organizations have other types of communication channels besides meetings available for use.

Traditional organizations are fond of extremely formal communication channels that follow the hierarchy of the organization, up and down the organization's structure, crossing lateral channels only at the highest hierarchical level. In such a rigid structure official communication typically takes place only through the senior administrative level. This obviously prohibits participation in the managerial process and inhibits input from all levels of the organization. The "grapevine" is usually thriving and is the major source of information for most employees.

In transitional organizations this rigid hierarchical structure needs to be broken up and official communication channels created at the middle management and desk levels with much of the information exchange or decision making taking place at the lowest possible authority level.

In every organization informal communication channels exist. They should be acknowledged and incorporated in the formal organization. Friends communicate suggested policy or organizational activities among themselves. This communication channel creates a network that is usually more efficient than the official channels though not always accurate. Managers can disseminate information through the informal channels by "depositing" it into the pipeline in seemingly casual remarks at staff gathering points or in conversations away from the workplace.

Upon initially joining an organization, assessing the interconnections and determining the informal network is essential. This network can benefit or harm the organization and effective utilization of the network can help the organization move toward its objectives. A better understanding of the informal communication channels can be gained through paying attention to the informal history of the organization and relationships between personnel.

QUALITY CIRCLES

Quality circles are considered the management tool of the 1970s and '80s. Used by Japanese companies since the early 1950s, they are thought to be largely responsible for the remarkable turnaround in the quality of Japan's industrial products. Their philosophy is based on the findings of American management experts like McGregor, Herzberg, and Likert, who promote democratic and humanistic management techniques.

According to Robert E. Cole, the six basic principles of quality circle activity are:

1. trust your employees
2. build employee loyalty to the company
3. invest in training and treat employees as resources which, if cultivated, will yield economic returns to the firm
4. recognize employee accomplishments
5. decentralize decision making
6. work should be seen as a cooperative effort with workers and managers doing the job together[2]

He defines quality circles as "a relatively autonomous unit composed of a small group of workers (ideally about 10), usually led by a foreman or senior worker and organized in each work unit. Participants are taught elementary techniques of problem solving including statistical methods. It is in principle a voluntary study group that concentrates on solving job-related quality problems." [3]

Skills necessary for creating effective quality circles include good human relations, analytical, decision-making, and motivational skills. Management has to trust in the ability of its employees to make a meaningful contribution toward solving organizational problems. But quality circles are a long-range, ongoing commitment. They are not designed to study one particular problem. Rather, they continuously scan the environment for opportunities to increase productivity or provide better service. That means management makes a long-term commitment to participation and employee development. Members of quality circles must trust and depend on each other, believing that their efforts are worthwhile and appreciated. Training in group dynamics and group decision-making processes is a necessary component of the implementation process.

Good analytical skills are rare and usually have to be developed in employees at all levels. Gathering information from coworkers (and not only those we know agree with us) regarding a problem, analyzing the underlying causes of problems (not just describing the problem), and finding new and innovative solutions are difficult tasks. Too often the process of defining a problem is hindered by premature closure. Some participants have already made up their minds about the causes of the problem and are unwilling to investigate deeper. Those members with a natural analytical bend are frustrated because they feel not all possibilities are adequately considered. Motivating different individuals to be willing to listen and probe, and knowing when to arrive at a decision are important skills, especially to the leader of a quality circle.

Decisions arrived at by quality circles will affect the work and lives of other employees and the organization as a whole. Being able to sell one's decision and gather support for its implementation are therefore crucial to a successful circle. Members must know how to make effective presentations, what tools to use to best make a point, and how to gear the presentation to the different audiences that usually need to be addressed.

Once problems are identified and analyzed, and decisions arrived at, recommendations need to be implemented. Training is necessary to assist quality circle members in motivating other employees and coworkers to try new approaches and give positive feedback to maintain the momentum. Unexpected problems always arise and need to be addressed in a detached, objective way so the end result is not lost in the frustrations of a momentary delay. The training necessary for quality circles is the training needed for all participatory endeavors.

Libraries, with their already highly educated staffs, may be excellent organizations to formally incorporate quality circles as a managerial tool. Managers who advocate their creation and provide the needed financial support show a commitment to creating a participatory environment in very tangible ways.

BUILDING ORGANIZATIONAL TRADITIONS

Creating a new organizational climate includes building new organizational traditions in addition to recognizing those already established. Annual retreats, staff appreciation events, Christmas and other holiday parties all help foster organizational cohesiveness and goodwill. They carry important symbolic messages to the staff and the greater environment, communicating an interest in participation, a caring for excellence, and a recognition of the social importance the work environment plays in individual's lives.

Retreats

Holding annual retreats for employees is an effective managerial tool for change in libraries. Retreats are useful to create a new organizational climate, help clarify organizational goals, improve overall communication, and involve all employees in the change process. During retreats managers and employees can communicate to the entire organization their vision for the organization and their trust in the ability of each other to realize this vision. Follow-up retreats can be used to measure organizational progress and provide positive feedback for accomplishments.

Employees of libraries in transition need to have time away from their usual responsibilities to consult, evaluate, reflect, and plan for the future. A consensus about where the organization is going has to be built, taking into consideration its history, resources, strengths, and weaknesses. Involving all staff in such an exercise gives the message that their opinions count and that their commitment to change is necessary and essential.

In discussion and planning sessions managers can assess how the organization views itself and if it is ready for a major change effort. Obstacles to change can be identified and their strengths measured against the necessity for and support of change. If a general consensus for changes evolves, implementation of specific strategies will be much more successful.

If possible, retreats should be held away from the library and last more than a day. A different location may stimulate creativity and fosters detachment from the daily activities and problems associated with work. Retreats usually build momentum. If only a day is devoted, the full emotional benefits that accrue by spending a considerable amount of time together with people from other divisions and departments cannot be harvested. Social activity will provide a bonding experience between many employees of the library which can then be used to facilitate organizational communication and problem solving.

Using in-house presenters and facilitators can provide library employees with a training ground to acquire or improve skills necessary in other settings. Employees will feel pleased to be chosen as presenters and have their expertise recognized by the entire organization. Colleagues from other libraries or institutions of higher education can be invited to share their ideas, experiences, or advice.

Retreats do not have to be expensive; local or in-house presenters can be used and most organizations have access to facilities away from the library at reasonable cost. Following an initially successful retreat, employees may even be willing to share part of the expenses by paying for their own meals or transportation.

Some general guidelines for retreats include:

- the more distance there is between the library and the retreat facility, the more useful retreats tend to be
- administrators and professional staff see more value in the retreat experience, preferring annual retreats
- biannual retreats appear to meet the needs of support staff
- if the retreat includes all staff, a survey of staff interests may be helpful to a committee charged with planning retreat activities
- continuing education activities may be included in retreats but should not be the entire focus
- social time is highly desirable and needs to be built into the retreat agenda
- retreat facilities should be pleasant and provide a comfortable setting for participants
- follow-up mechanisms need to be established to ensure that retreat recommendations are implemented and participants receive adequate feedback

Retreats may be especially helpful in libraries undergoing a leadership transition. They can be a very effective way for a new director to get to know the library's staff, while the staff can find out the directions the library is likely to move in and what role the director wants them to play in the organization.

Staff Appreciation Ceremonies

Creating a special event to recognize the accomplishments of library staff will provide many intangible, yet long-lasting, benefits for both organization and employees. The fact that staff are important enough to be officially recognized for their efforts on a periodic basis builds loyalty and organizational commitment. Although most library employees are highly motivated and self-directed, the extra recognition by and before peers provides an additional incentive to perform well.

In libraries in transition it is advisable to let staff themselves choose those employees they perceive to be meritorious and deserving of special recognition. This approach will again tell staff that management trusts them to know best who the outstanding performers are. In addition, staff itself proclaim to the organization through their choices what their performance expectations are and who meets or exceeds those expectations.

In addition to recognizing outstanding performers, managers can select employees who set examples in other ways. Years of service and perfect attendance awards, efforts toward physical fitness, etc., can be used to show appreciation for loyalty, commitment, and self-improvement. Tokens of appreciation in the form of certificates, plaques, pins, are very important and carry the feelings of recognition and belonging into the future. The appendix includes an example of a staff recognition policy. Inviting employees' families and friends to staff appreciation activities will increase the impact of recognition received. It will help build a supportive relationship between the staff members' work and other important areas of their lives.

Employee Assistance Programs: A Positive Approach to the Problem Employee.*

What Are EAPs?

Employee assistance programs (EAPs) are management tools that address work performance problems. EAPs address personal problems, often psychological or addictive in nature. A strong relationship among major personal problems, productivity, and general job performance has become increasingly evident. In the past, personal problems were not considered when resolving personnel matters. Since in a service and information society, workers, rather than machines and equipment, are the most important assets of an employer, management realizes that it is more humane as well as more cost-effective to the organization to help employees resolve personal conflicts and resume a productive career.

Libraries, facing the same personnel issues as other organizations, may want to identify available counseling services, such as EAPs, within the parent organization and explore their use to help employees cope with automation, new service demands, changes in managerial styles, funding cutbacks, burnout, and changes in worker expectations.

Development of EAPs

The beginnings of employee assistance programs can be traced to 1917 when Macy's department store established a counseling service to help employees resolve personal problems. By the 1930s and 1940s, companies had established problem-specific assistance programs such as those designed to rehabilitate alcoholics. Gradually the focus of these assistance programs broadened into personal counseling within the workplace, dealing with alcoholism, drug abuse, family problems, financial/legal programs, emotional problems, health-related problems, and stress. In the past, most organizations, including libraries, responded to individual problems with anger, frustration, confusion, ambivalence, or sympathy, hoping that family, church, and community would assist them. When work deficiencies became unacceptable, the employee was most often terminated or the problem ignored.

---

*This article by Webb and Cargill is reprinted here (up to page 108, "Training Needs,") with the permission of the American Library Association. It was originally published in the *LAMA Newsletter,* vol. 12, no. 13, June 1986, pp. 65–68.

According to Alan Edwards, "counseling can be compared to getting help for a physical problem from a physician."[1] Supervisors, as well as the population at large, are not trained to correctly diagnose and address personal problems. Speculation and assumptions about the causes of problems are usually counterproductive, even harmful.

Professional counseling has, therefore, become an acceptable avenue for objectively examining difficulties that individuals experience and helps people acquire constructive coping skills for a changing environment. Provisions of assistance within the workplace may also become a method for coping with increased insurance costs within the next decade and may become mandatory in the future. The knowledge that problems are a part of everyone's life and the acceptability of counseling as a constructive means to face and work out problems has encouraged the growth of EAPs.

Different Ways to Establish EAPs

Employee assistance programs may exist with two different approaches to resolving problems: preventive and confrontational. The preventive approach is aimed at the employee who needs assistance before a problem has an impact on job performance. The confrontational approach is utilized when an employee has performance deficiencies that must be addressed and resolved.

Utilization of EAPs may also be voluntary or mandatory. With the voluntary approach, a supervisor may identify surfacing problems and suggest an employee seek trained counseling assistance, or the employee may recognize on his or her own the need for help. With mandatory referrals, an employee is required to seek assistance as a means of retaining employment.

Employee assistance programs may also be external or internal. A hot line, offering minimal problem and referral assistance, is one model that primarily provides crisis intervention and serves as a conduit to more in-depth counseling services.

Several agencies may have counseling assistance provided as part of a consortium arrangement. Similarly, EAPs may be contractual in nature, providing services to employees of specific organizations. These three external models—hot line, consortium, or contractual—have the advantages of confidentiality, counselor expertise, and off-site counseling.

Internal models may assume different forms but a common trait is on-site access. One model has the EAP office on the employer's premises. A second model has counseling services offered on the employer's site but also utilizes referrals to off-site services. A third model is managerial hierarchy of a director or coordinator with counselors offering services at different locations within the organization. There may also be union-based EAPs.

Responsibilities of Different Components in the Work Setting

Without top management's financial and moral support, EAPs could not return employees to productive work. This support needs to be constantly communicated to workers and middle management through training workshops, publications, and testimonials. Supervisors are the backbone of an EAP since they deal with employees on a day-to-day basis and can recognize the signs of deteriorating job performance.

Labor's long-term support for treating alcoholism through EAPs spurred their growth. With the changes in the work force from predominantly blue- to white-collar, unions became supportive of "broad brush" EAPs that address all kinds of personal problems. Union officials, trained to recognize work problems before they become insurmountable, can become allies of management and supervisors by encouraging problem workers to seek assistance through EAPs. Unions help guarantee that employees referred to an EAP receive fair and equitable treatment at work while under care.

Feinstein and Brown list the following signs to watch for in problem workers: chronic absenteeism, change in behavior, physical signs, spasmodic work pace, lower quantity and quality of work, partial absences, lying, avoiding supervisors and coworkers, on-the-job accidents, lost time due to on-the-job accidents, and lost time due to off-the-job accidents. They also suggest steps for supervisors to correct performance problems before they become unmanageable:

1. Verify that the employee's performance is deteriorating as evidenced by precise documentation.
2. Limit criticism to overall job performance and avoid trying to diagnose the employee's underlying problem.
3. Document examples of poor job performance. Be specific and factual regarding the date, time, place, and nature of the incidents.
4. Discuss all aspects of the problem with the immediate supervisor.
5. Arrange for a confidential interview with the employee. Discuss the poor work performance and make it clear that if work performance is not improved, disciplinary action will be taken.
6. Suggest that the employee visit the employee assistance program to discuss the problem that is adversely affecting job performance.
7. If job performance continues to deteriorate and the employee refuses all offers of help, denies the problem, or does not cooperate or respond to treatment, then appropriate disciplinary action should be taken.[2]

According to Alan Edwards, supervisors must have good communication skills and promote an openness with employees.[3] However, supervisors must be careful not to encourage problem workers to continue deteriorating performance by offering misguided sympathy. They must respect the dignity of a troubled employee, practice confidentiality concerning the problem, and if possible, change work assignments to more structured, non-decision-making tasks. If reassignment is not an option, joint decision making may be undertaken. Management styles may be changed to provide troubled workers with more or less support, depending on the situation.

The counselor's role is pivotal in the reintegration of the employee into the workplace. A good trust relationship between counselors and employees will often encourage coworkers to utilize EAPs even before problems are apparent. Counseling staff of EAPs must be accessible, respect confidentiality, be trained in counseling and able to assess and diagnose the problem, be aware of referral services, understand the role of the EAP within the organization, be responsible and aware of legal and ethical principles, and have management support.

Services the EAP staff can provide include providing feedback to the employer about job modification or other changes needed, assisting with job redesign, training supervisors in identifying problems to refer to EAP, carrying out career evaluation and development.

Legal Issues

According to William A. Carnahan, the legal counselor of the Association of Labor-Management Administrators and Consultants on Alcoholism, legal issues concerning EAPs focus primarily on governmental regulations and labor-management liabilities.[4] These include licensing treatment personnel, licensing treatment facilities, and requiring confidentiality of patient records. It is irrelevant whether the services are provided on an in-house basis or contracted out, since all health-related licensing requirements are applicable to EAPs.

Labor/management liabilities are more complex and difficult. Issues at stake are the employer's responsibility to ensure EAP access, the extent to which employers or unions are liable for an adverse outcome if an employee participates at the behest of his employer (or union), and the appropriate disciplinary sanctions used by an employer should an employee decline to participate in an EAP or should rehabilitation be unsuccessful.

The responsibility of an employer to actively encourage employee participation in EAPs is well established. Such encouragement takes the form of leave time and job security during the time of rehabilitation. Employees are not required to pay for the cost of treatment; in most cases these are covered through insurance benefits.

Employees unhappy with EAPs have most often claimed breach of confidentiality, negligence, and wrong treatment. To protect EAP staff against such allegations, employers with EAP programs must acquire professional liability insurance for the EAP employees.

Generally, disciplinary actions by employers must wait until an employee proves a failure to rehabilitate after more than one try. However, a proper dismissal is in order if the employer can show a policy of forbearance, offer of and encouragement for treatment, a final notice that the job is in jeopardy, and lack of progress by the employee.

The right of employers to require employees to submit to urinalysis to detect the presence of drugs or alcohol has been held by the courts and will assist employers in referring problem employees to EAPs with a decreased risk of liability. Drug testing is becoming more prevalent in today's society.

Cost Benefits

Measuring the effectiveness of EAP programs is as problematic as evaluating all human service programs designed to partially achieve humanitarian goals. Most employers, however, have expectations of improved productivity and monetary savings. The literature on EAPs presents numerous case studies estimating the cost savings achieved, taking into account tangible and intangible benefits attributed to EAP intervention.

Current cost in lost productivity from alcoholism alone is estimated by Kemp to be $42.75 billion per year, while the cost of drug abuse is another $40 billion per year.[5] According to McClellan, industrial stress accounts for an additional $32 billion loss annually in work-related accidents and contributes to heart disease, which in turn is responsible for an annual loss of more than 135 million workdays.[6] Advocates of EAPs most often cite reduced absenteeism, improved morale, less turnover, fewer injurious accidents and deaths, reduced insurance rates, fewer grievances, and reduced recruitment costs as benefits that can be substantiated through case studies.

At Alcoa, for example, net savings from reduced absenteeism alone—a reduction by 58 percent—paid for the EAP program. A study by Featherston and Bednarek shows that savings through an EAP at a hospital with about 1,000 employees amounted to $72,228 per year as a result of employees returning to work, as opposed to the costs of terminating them and paying separation pay, recruiting and training new employees, and lowering unemployment and health insurance costs.[7] An evaluation of the EAP services at Anheuser-Busch revealed that 87 percent of employees who had used the EAP found it helpful. Almost half of the users (46 percent) probably would not have sought assistance if there hadn't been an EAP and if users knew of a fellow employee with difficulties; 84 percent indicated that they would or probably would recommend EAP services.

Kemp[8] reported returns on investments for state EAPs at ratios from 1:3 to 1:8 depending on the type of program used. Benefits will start to accrue after two years or more, because initially, referred workers have problems that developed over many years that will not disappear miraculously. The impact on lowering medical costs and insurance rates will increase with the longevity of an EAP, as its focus changes from rehabilitation to prevention.

Ten to 15 percent of the employee population needs counseling at any given time, according to Kemp. Personal problems become the concern of companies when they affect the employees' work performance. EAPs appear to be a means of addressing problems caused by alcoholism, drug abuse, stress, divorce, mental illness, bankruptcy, grief, etc. More than half of the largest 500 industries now have EAPs, with an estimated 5,500 programs in the private sector, according to Kemp.[9] In the public sector, the federal government is the leader in establishing EAPs. This growth attests to the increasing need to address performance problems and a change in employer's philosophies away from viewing personal problems as separate from work life.

Limitations of EAPs

There are limitations on the use of EAPs. Some of these rest with the supervisor who may be inadequately trained to refer employees to the program or who may be reluctant to utilize it. Management may also fail to allow adequate time for an EAP to develop, achieve recognition, and become effective.

There are limitations within the EAPs themselves. While they treat the symptoms that lead to the performance dysfunction, they may fail to address the underlying problem that led to the symptoms that in turn led to dysfunction. The emphasis is on resolving the evident weakness that is causing on-the-job problems, yet the root cause may be ignored. EAPs may also be designed to deal with only a few problems rather than with the interdependence of problems.

When to Use an EAP

As already discussed, supervisors are the most important link between employees and EAPs. They are in an excellent position to spot behavior changes, excessive leave usage, and deteriorating work performance. Not all performance or attendance problems should, however, be automatically referred to an EAP. Only cases where poor or inconsistent job performance continues after the supervisor has addressed the issue should be referred.

EAP counselors and management should develop appropriate supervisory training to sensitize supervisors to the symptoms of alcoholism and other behavioral problems. Care must be taken that EAP referrals are based on documented work performance deficiencies. Supervisors should beware of getting involved with employees' personal problems. Excessive sympathy may encourage performance problems; destructive compassion prevents the employee from facing the problem or looking for solutions. Libraries may also want to consider using EAPs for stress reduction sessions and to diffuse long-standing personality conflicts.

The positive results and growth of EAPs generally indicate their effectiveness in addressing work performance problems in a humanistic way. As Dickman and Ememer point out, when organizations help their employees with their personal problems, the organizations are ultimately helping themselves.[10] The benefits are felt not only by employees and employers but also by better-functioning families and the community at large. Library management has changed—and is changing—just as managerial styles at large have changed. Libraries should adopt management tools that have proven effective in other organizations and use them to their benefit.

1. Alan Edwards. "Just Down or Out? Helping Troubled Employees." *Supervisory Management* 29 (June 1984): 10–12.

2. Barbara Feinstein and Edwin G. Brown. *New Partnership: Human Services with Business and Industry* (Cambridge, MA: Schenkmann Publishing Co., 1982).

3. Edwards, pp. 10–12.

4. William A. Carnahan. *Legal Issues Affecting Employee Assistance Programs* (Arlington, VA: The Association of Labor-Management Administrators and Consultants on Alcoholism, Inc., 1984).

5. Donna R. Kemp. "State Employee Assistance Programs: Organization and Services." *Public Administration Review* 45 (May-June 1985): 378–82.

6. Keith McClellan. "Changing Nature of EAP Practice." *Personnel Administrator* 30 (August 1985): 29–37.

7. H. Joe Featherston and Robert J. Bednarek. "A Positive Demonstration of Concern for Employees." *Personnel Administrator* 26 (September 1981): 43–47.

8. Kemp, pp. 378–82.

9. Kemp, pp. 378–82.

10. J. Fred Dickman, G. William Ememer, Jr., and William S. Hutchison, Jr. *Counseling the Troubled Person in Industry: A Guide to the Organization, Implementation, and Evaluation of Employee Assistance Programs* (Springfield, IL: Charles C. Thomas, 1985).

TRAINING NEEDS

Because of the increased training needs of changing organizations, companies that produce management and training films, videocassettes, and audiocassettes are proliferating in the United States. A selected bibliography of audiovisual materials that the authors found helpful in their own work as managers in transitional libraries appears at the end of the book, prior to the appendix. The materials can also be used to start or support staff development programs. Many state libraries provide such audiovisual materials on loan.

NOTES

1. George E. Vaillant. *Adaptation to Life* (Boston: Little, Brown and Company, 1977).
2. Robert E. Cole, "Learning from the Japanese: Prospects and Pitfalls," in chapter 1 of *Quality Circles: Selected Readings,* eds. Robert W. Berger and David L. Shores (New York: Marcel Dekker, Inc., 1986, p. 39).
3. Robert E. Cole. "Learning from the Japanese: Prospects and Pitfalls." *Management Review* 69 (September 1980): 22-42.

PART III

Using Human Resources to Implement and Manage Change

Chapter 7
Creating a Staff for a Changing Library

Managers in changing libraries are building a new organizational culture. They accomplish this by developing existing human resources and by hiring new employees whose philosophies are already compatible with the new organizational norms.

HIRING NEW EMPLOYEES

Within a changing library organization the hiring of new employees can be one of the most important steps toward increasing the change in momentum. In addition to vacancies created by normal turnover, positions will be opening up because a minority of employees will decide to leave, not being willing to make the necessary adjustments as changes take place.

Management should expect that the need to hire new employees to replace those that depart for whatever reason will be perceived by some people either within the library or elsewhere as a clear indication of dissatisfaction and poor management. There are always individuals who feel that a stable, long-term staff with little or no turnover is a sign of a sound, well-functioning organization and that an organization that has frequent turnover, especially after a managerial change, is an organization that is unstable and in the throes of upheaval.

When vacancies do occur, immediate hiring of a replacement with the same job description as his or her predecessor is too often an automatic, routine, and easy-to-implement step. This should not be the procedure, however. What should be the automatic routine step is to conduct a job analysis.

Job Analysis

Organizations get accustomed to functioning with a certain number of employees in specific classifications or rankings who are thought to be absolutely essential to the accomplishment of stated or assumed goals. With change efforts underway within an organization, the traditional mission and goals of a library invariably change, too. It is, therefore, an essential first step to request an historical analysis of each vacated position, no matter if it is classified as a professional or support staff position. Questions to be asked within the historical analysis include:

- When was the position originally created?
- Who was the first person to hold that position?
- What qualifications were previously needed for the position?
- Which position, in which department, was responsible for the duties of that position before it was created?
- Is the position necessary to achieve the new goals of the organization?
- How does the position fit into the overall organizational structure?
- Does it need to be filled at the same level?
- Who could assume the responsibilities if it was not filled?
- What are the qualifications needed as the position is now envisioned?

Requiring a thorough position analysis for each vacancy will serve to communicate once again the new goals of the organization. It will force supervisors and administrators to rethink workflow and staffing levels. If a supervisor insists on filling the position at the previous level without changes, the manager has several choices. He or she can:

- comply with the supervisor's wishes
- insist that changes be made
- restate the guidelines for the analysis, have the supervisor conduct a second analysis, and hope that the supervisor will arrive at a different conclusion the second time
- leave the position vacant for a period of time

Part of managing an organization in transition is to teach the existing staff how to make the transition, lead them to think in terms of change, and inspire them to focus on change in general. Thus, a manager might very well choose the fourth alternative of leaving the position vacant for a period of time in order to let the supervisor and the manager have the opportunity to observe how work is redistributed during the interim, what tasks cannot be assumed by others, and how well a unit functions without it.

Ideally the entire work unit should be involved in analyzing each vacancy so that each member of the unit can become informed about the responsibilities of the position and can appreciate the interrelationship of the vacant position with their own work. This is the time to decide if the position really merits the qualifications of a professional or if a highly skilled support staff member could perform most of the responsibilities. As the workforce is becoming more educated, libraries and librarians need to identify and define clearly the truly professional responsibilities of a librarian and assign other duties to support staff with equally valuable areas of expertise.

Shortly after assuming his new assistant director position, David Norris was faced with the resignation of a librarian in the exchange unit of the library. On his interview David had clearly stated that whenever he had a vacancy, he would require that a job analysis be done before hiring a replacement. However, Nora Ruff, the supervisor of the department of which the exchange unit was a part, immediately came to David when she learned of the resignation of the exchange librarian and presented a list of potential members of the search committee, a list of candidates for the position, and a copy of the job description for the exchange librarian.

When David reminded her of the need for a job analysis and presented her with the questions he wanted answered in the course of conducting the job analysis, Nora was insistent that the position be filled immediately. David informed her that the position could remain vacant for the foreseeable future, instructed her to reassign the duties of the exchange librarian, and gave Nora a deadline for submitting a completed job analysis.

When the deadline came, Nora presented David with an analysis that justified retention of the exchange librarian position. David sensed that Nora had not truly conducted an analysis but had simply justified the retention of a librarian position reporting to her. He had often heard Nora bragging about the number and levels of staff under her supervision.

David asked Nora to analyze the position again and provided her with more detailed guidelines including consideration of different levels of staffing. When the second analysis was submitted, David found that Nora had reassigned the duties of the exchange librarian to other staff within the department and had suggested that the salary for the position be given to herself and others as raises.

****

Do you think David acted appropriately? What would you have done differently? Can Nora be considered a change agent? What were her major concerns? Were they legitimate?

Job Description

Once a job analysis has been completed, and it has been determined that the position will be filled, then a decision must be made concerning the staffing level; for example, what level it will be assigned within a classification system. Next, the position description should be drafted.

The writing of a relevant job description should be relatively easy after the completion of a thorough job analysis. Whether it is for a professional or support position, the position description generally includes the following elements:

- functional area of the position
- position title
- position level
- position purpose
- position dimension
- principle duties
- supervision given and received
- qualifications required and desired
- accountability

The statement of <u>functional area of the position</u> should give an applicant an indication of where the position falls within the library: Is it a public service, technical service, or senior administrative position?

The <u>position title</u> should be meaningful and reflect the responsibilities accurately when compared with similar positions in the library. The title of Assistant Director of Libraries for Administrative Services, for example, should mean that the position is primarily concerned with administrative responsibilities, including budgeting and personnel. If titles are too vague or too elaborate to convey the sense of what the job is all about, chances are good that an unsuitable choice will be made to fill the vacancy.

The <u>position level</u> should clearly indicate whether the position is that of a degreed librarian or of a support staff member. The <u>position purpose</u> should indicate the importance of the position to the organization. It, like the <u>position dimension</u> statement, should inform applicants about the main areas of responsibilities assigned to the position.

<u>Principle duties</u> include a more detailed list of the tasks for which the position holder is responsible and on which evaluations will be based. The job description should be specific about the amount of <u>supervision given and received</u> for the position. <u>Qualifications required and desired</u> should be specific and non-discriminatory. Only qualifications that are essential to the fulfillment of responsibilities should be included as required. Preferred or desired qualifications may be included but cannot be used as the sole criteria for hiring. Lastly, the job description should generally define the level of <u>accountability</u> and performance criteria used in evaluating position holders. Ahead are two examples of position announcements/descriptions—one for a clerical position and the other for a professional librarian position.

Figure 1. Clerical Position Announcement/Description

General Description:
    A clerical position involving work with specialized and technical library tasks and the public.

Scope of Duties and Responsibilities:
    Responsibilities include technical activities such as operation of OCLC library computer system, operation of microcomputers, operation of CLSI library circulation computer system, operation of mailing machinery, and other departmental equipment. Duties include recordkeeping involved with serials aspect of gifts and exchange program, supervising of clericals who build records on OCLC, research on serials received through gifts and exchange program, and library mail and delivery services. Work is performed with some verbal and written supervision augmented with independent judgments based on training. Employee performance is based upon review of completed work and overall results obtained.

Supervisory Responsibilities:
    Supervises student assistants and other clerical employees as needed.

Examples of Work Performed:
- Receive gifts and exchange items for the library.
- Acknowledge gifts received.
- Supervise mailing of exchange materials.
- Request claims for missing materials.
- Bibliographic work on serials items on OCLC library computer system.
- Build local records on OCLC.
- Train and supervise clericals who build local records on OCLC.
- Research information on title changes for serials.
- Correct serials information on OCLC.
- Work on microcomputers and CLSI library circulation system.
- Assist patrons on the telephone and in person.
- Assist in mail and deliveries for library.

Required Knowledge, Abilities, and Skills:
- Knowledge of office practices and methods.
- Ability to operate office machines and microcomputers.
- Ability to deal effectively with people.
- Ability to work with others, to train and give instructions.
- Ability to perform mathematical calculations and/or verify information accurately.

Minimum Acceptable Training and Skills:
- Proficiency in written and mathematical skills as may be reflected in the completion of high school.
- Prefer three years of office experience with progressively more responsibility, preferably with some library experience.
- Additional education may substitute for the required experience on a year-for-year basis.
- Minimum typing speed of 40 words per minute.

Desirable Knowledge and Skills:
    Ability to do library research with training.

HIRING SUPPORT STAFF

Although their importance is increasing rapidly in libraries, support staff positions are still filled on a local or regional basis. Many libraries will first advertise in-house to give current employees the opportunity to apply. If no suitable in-house candidate is found, the library's parent organization, be it the university, the city, or county, will most likely advertise and screen prospective employees.

When hiring support staff, the library will generally list the position with the parent organization's personnel department. The vacancy will then be listed on a telephone job line, with the city or state employment departments, or on a centrally located bulletin board. How the position vacancy is made known will vary with different organizations.

As applications are received, those meeting the position criteria will be selected for potential interviews. Care should be taken to select only those applicants that meet the required qualifications, such as typing skill levels or computer expertise. Employment history should be reviewed. Applicants should then be called and interviews scheduled. When applicants for support positions are called for interviews, the following information should be relayed:

- The person calling should clearly state his or her name, the name of the library, and the purpose for the call.
- The caller should then ask if the applicant is free to talk at that particular moment.
- The type of position available should be identified, as well as its level and salary, and when it will be available.
- Some details of the responsibilities of the job should be given.
- The caller should then ask if the applicant would like to interview for the position.
- If an interview time is set, the caller should be sure that the applicant knows where to go for the interview and who will be conducting the interview.
- The caller should also ask the applicant if references can be contacted.

If the library has a personnel office, it is a good idea for the applicant to be directed to that office first. Then a member of the personnel staff can provide the applicant with a copy of the position description, escort the applicant to the interview location, and introduce the applicant to the staff conducting the interview.

How the interview process is handled can influence the applicant's opinion of the organization. The interview process needs to be an example of fairness and equal opportunity. When planning the interview for a support staff vacancy, more than one person should conduct the interview if at all possible. The individuals involved should be those who will be working closely with the person in the position. The department supervisor should communicate the following points with the individuals who will be conducting the interviews:

- The interviews need to be conducted in a quiet, private place.
- The interviewers should become familiar with affirmative action/equal employment opportunity guidelines, including the types of questions that are inappropriate.
- Those people conducting the interview should have a written list of questions that will be asked of all applicants.
- The hiring recommendation should be prepared a certain way for the supervisor.
- The people conducting the interview should make no job offers in the course of the interview.

Careful planning of the interview process will help ensure—though not guarantee—that problems won't arise later. For support staff positions, the length of interviews will vary with the importance of the position, ranging from 30 minutes for a basic clerical position to a day for specialist positions in automation, personnel, and accounting.

After the interviews are completed, the hiring recommendation should include the following elements:

- be in written form so it can become a part of the permanent file on the hiring decision
- state how many applicants were interviewed
- indicate which applicants met which required qualifications for the position
- indicate qualifications the applicants did not meet
- clearly state why the recommended person for the position was chosen

References should be called to confirm the applicant's qualifications and skills for the job.

When the successful applicant for the position is called, he or she should be told the desired starting date. If notice must be given to a current employer, this date may have to be negotiated. The procedure to be followed on the first day on the job, such as obtaining a parking permit or reporting first to the personnel office, should be spelled out. As quickly as possible, the unsuccessful applicants should be notified. If there were internal candidates for the job, they should be contacted first. Outside candidates should be informed that they were not selected so they can seek positions elsewhere.

Any required personnel transaction forms should be completed immediately so that the new employee is listed on the payroll. Time sheets and other required forms should be prepared for the new employee. Instruction in completing these forms and the schedule for turning them in should be covered when the new employee arrives to work.

RECRUITMENT FOR PROFESSIONAL VACANCIES

Hiring for professional positions is more complex than selection of individuals for support positions. An involved recruitment process is usually followed in the hiring process for librarians. Most libraries have an internal policy to recruit nationally for all professional positions. Establishing such a policy may be a necessity for libraries in transition because they often want to recruit experts to facilitate anticipated change. Having such a policy does not mean that the organization prefers outsiders; it merely emphasizes that it is interested in hiring the best librarian for the job, whether he or she comes from a pool of internal or external candidates.

Figure 2. Professional Librarian Position Announcement/Description

Title:	Head, Bibliographic Control
Duties:	Responsible for the effective and efficient operation of the Bibliographic Control Department with its authority, inventory, verification, cataloging, and classification functions. Responsible for all aspects of personnel management including selection, supervision, motivation, and evaluation of librarians, support staff, and student assistants. Ensures that internal policies are consistent with national, state, university, and librarywide standards and guidelines. Formulates policy for Bibliographic Control. Plans for incorporation of technologies into cataloging and classification functions. Develops effective functional relationships between the Bibliographic Control Department and other library areas. Reports to the Associate Director of Libraries for Information Access and Systems.
Requirements:	Master's degree from an ALA-accredited library school; second master's degree desirable. Minimum of five years (most recent five) of Library of Congress cataloging experience. At least three years of successful supervisory experience. Extensive knowledge of national cataloging and classification codes, rules, and standards. Experience with OCLC or other bibliographic utility. Knowledge of foreign languages. Record of participation in professional associations at the national level. Ability to lead organizational change in a dynamic environment.
Salary/Benefits:	Salary $25,000–$30,000 for a 12-month appointment. Excellent benefits package; 88% of Social Security paid for first $16,500 of salary; choice of retirement programs including TIAA-CREF; 14 state holidays; no state or local income tax.
General Inform.:	The University is one of five comprehensive state universities in the state and has an enrollment of 24,000. It is located in a commercial center for the area with a metropolitan population of 224,000. The library has 1.1 million volumes and a materials budget of 1.7 million. Planning for an online catalog is underway.

Application: Applications received prior to May 31, 1988 will be given first consideration. Position available immediately. Send a statement with your application summarizing the role of a Bibliographic Control Department in an academic library. Send letter of application, resume, statement, names, and address of three references to the Assistant Director of Libraries for Personnel Services. Minorities are encouraged to apply.

An initial step in the recruitment process is the writing and placement of an advertisement in appropriate periodicals. These periodicals will include professional journals and other publications aimed at the type of organization of which the library is a part, such as *The Chronicle of Higher Education* for positions in academic libraries.

A one-page flyer with the position description can be prepared and mailed to library schools and to other libraries. Its display may elicit applications for the position in addition to those applications received as a result of the advertisements. Copies of the complete position description should be available to be mailed to applicants. The advertisements and the flyers should include:

- a succinct description of the position
- the application deadline
- to whom the application should be directed
- what constitutes a complete application: for example, a letter; a copy of the applicant's resume; names, addresses, and phone numbers of references; and, for some positions, a philosophical statement

Search Committees

In libraries in transition, search committees are an excellent means to involve staff in hiring decisions. Search committees educate staff about the availability of viable applicants, build support for newly hired employees, and create an awareness of the difficult decisions inherent in filling a position. Seldom is there only one person who can meet the job requirements. When in-house applicants are considered, committee members are forced to make many professional and ethical decisions to deal with the subtle or not so subtle pressures applied to their already difficult task. It is very helpful to search committees to have their charges and responsibilities well defined. The committee should also be apprised of the fact that ethical, professional conduct is expected of members of the search committee. A charge to a search committee for a managerial position might read as follows:

Figure 3. Search Committee Memo

DATE: September 1, 1987

TO: Members of the Search Committee for (name of position)
(list of members of the committee)

FROM: (Head of Reference)

RE: Search Committee Charge

Thank you for agreeing to serve on this Search Committee. The deadline for applications is November 30. My secretary will contact each of you and schedule the first meeting of the committee. I will meet with you briefly at the initial meeting to discuss and clarify the charge to the committee, outline the search procedure, and answer any questions. At the initial committee meeting, you should also be prepared to elect a committee chair.

The Charge:
Your charge is to recommend to me the two or three persons who would, in the committee's judgment, best fill this position. Though I will make the final decision of whom to recommend to the Director, your assistance in the screening process is critical.

Many of the responsibilities formerly within the purview of a Search Committee are now handled by the Personnel Officer, thus freeing the Search Committee to concentrate on screening, interviewing, and evaluating. Among the responsibilities that will be handled by the Personnel Officer are: writing and placing the advertisement; ensuring that affirmative action guidelines are followed; receiving and acknowledging applications; and keeping applicants informed of the status of their applications.

Responsibilities that are associated with the charge to the search committee include, but are not limited to: reviewing applications; recommending top candidates for interviews; coordinating the scheduling of visits by the candidates; making final committee recommendations of the top two or three candidates, in unranked order, to me; and generally conducting the search process in a professional manner.

As you review applications and interview and evaluate candidates, please keep in mind that this is a key managerial position in the organization, and we seek a cooperative person with a positive, forward-looking attitude, an individual who will be supportive of the direction in which the organization is moving.

The Search Process:
We want to ensure that the search process is conducted in an ethical manner. To that end, I am outlining some of what I consider to be elements of an effective, fair search procedure.

1. A requirement for this position is a one-page statement of the philosophy of the role this position will play in the organization. If applicants do not include this, they should be reminded to submit one.
2. The Personnel Officer will receive the applications. The committee should review the applicants' letters, resumes, and philosophical statements and inform the Personnel Officer of the ones for which the committee wants letters of reference requested.
3. Telephone interviews can be used for screening purposes if the committee wishes. Candidates should be contacted before the telephone interview so the interview can be scheduled at the convenience of the committee and the candidate.
4. The Personnel Officer and I should be notified of the candidates selected for interviewing; we will review your selections and affirm that the candidates meet the qualification requirements.

5. When the interview schedule is created, it should include the following elements:
   —a session with the Director, midway through the interview;
   —an initial hour session with me early in the interview; a social period (dinner) with me; and an hour and a half with me near the end of the interview;
   —a group interview with the departmental staff;
   —a group interview opportunity for the entire library;
   —a session with the Personnel Officer near the end of the interview.
6. If problems or conflicts arise during the search process and the committee cannot handle them, please inform the Personnel Officer or me so we can intervene. Harrassment of candidates, including inappropriate questioning of them, is unacceptable. Also, please observe strict confidentiality.
7. Do not call people the candidate has not designated as references within the candidate's home institution *without* telling him or her you will be doing so. You could unintentionally create grave problems for the candidate.
8. The search committee should determine what rating method or mechanism for staff input will be used.
9. The search committee should forward to me, after the interviews, the two or three applicants who, in the committee's judgment, would best fill the position, listing the pluses and minuses of each candidate.
10. I will then make the final recommendation to the Director, offer the position, and discharge the committee after the offer is accepted.

A copy of the position description is attached.

Figure 4. Head, Bibliographic Control Position Description

AREA: Information Access and Systems
POSITION TITLE: Head, Bibliographic Control
DATE PREPARED: December 1987

Position Purpose:
A key library managerial position to direct the activities associated with identifying, describing, and classifying information and materials, acquired for the Libraries' collections, to facilitate access by students, faculty, and other users.

Dimension:
Responsible for all aspects of cataloging and classifying library materials. During the course of these activities, interacts with all areas within Information Access and Systems. Manages a staff consisting of both professional librarians and support staff. Is in contact with other university units, students, faculty, staff, and local community members in the process of organizing materials.

Principle Duties:
1. Responsible for the effective and efficient operation of the Bibliographic Control Department with its authority, inventory, verification, cataloging, and classification functions. Assumes a leadership role within department and library organization.
2. Responsible for all aspects of personnel management in the Bibliographic Control Department including selection, supervision, motivation, and evaluation of librarians, support staff, and student assistants.
3. Makes ultimate decisions on cataloging rule and policy interpretations.
4. Ensures that internal policies are consistent with national, state, university, and librarywide standards and guidelines.

5. Formulates policy for Bibliographic Control Department.
6. Plans for incorporation of technologies into cataloging and classifying functions, working closely with Automation Coordinator.
7. Encourages and provides continued opportunities for self and staff to develop professionally.
8. Develops effective functional relationships between Bibliographic Control Department and other library areas.
9. Sets the tone for positive and effective communication among staff members.
10. Pursues library funding from sources other than State appropriations.
11. Participates in collection development program by providing supportive analysis of collection through statistics.
12. May participate in collection development as a liaison.
13. Prepares requested reports.

Supervision:
Received: Responsible to the Associate Director of Libraries for Information Access and Systems. Given: To librarians, library assistants, and student assistants within department.

Qualifications:
- ALA-accredited Master of Library Science required.
- Second Master's desirable.
- Formal or continuing education in supervision and management desirable.
- Extensive knowledge of national cataloging and classification codes, rules and standards.
- Minimum of five years (most recent five) of Library of Congress cataloging experience.
- Minimum of three years of successful supervisory experience.
- Experience with OCLC or other major bibliographic utility.
- Knowledge of foreign languages.
- Possess high-quality oral and written communication skills.
- Record of participation in professional associations and contributions to the profession at national levels.
- An understanding of and commitment to the use of computing and other technologies in the cataloging function.
- Demonstrated skills in personnel management, communication, leadership, and ability to motivate staff.

Accountability:
Accountable for setting organizational objectives and evaluated by how well objectives are met.

If the library has a personnel office, as in the above case, much of the support work, like the advertisements, letters of receipt of applications, reference checks, rejection letters, and offers to applicants, can be carried out by that office. If there is no personnel office, the committee will have to handle these duties as well. If that is the case, the committee should be sure that all aspects of the paperwork required are carried out in a timely manner. As each application is received, it should be acknowledged and a full position description sent to the applicant. When the list of people to be interviewed is compiled and the interviews are scheduled, information on the library and the city in which it is located should be forwarded to each candidate.

The Interview

The Personnel Officer will serve as a resource person to a search committee or supervisor during the entire interview process. He or she can advise on the legality and appropriateness of interview questions, troubleshoot when problems start to develop, and be responsible for all written communication between candidates and the library. Before candidates are invited for interviews, the personnel office should check references. In addition to those references given directly by the candidate, the personnel office, after informing the candidate, may also want to check if academic credentials were actually earned as stated and try to talk to current and previous supervisors of candidates to determine their suitability for the advertised position.

For professional positions, interviews usually will last at least one day but can take as long as a week if a director is to be hired. Changing organizations should try to involve as many people as possible in the interview process in order to receive as much input as possible about candidates' qualities and qualifications.

The interview sessions with the search committee should be structured and address qualifications, professional background, professional interests, special skills, and abilities necessary for the position. The same questions should be asked of each candidate and responses written down for comparison at a later time. The search committee can also ask sensitive questions that it knows staff want answered but may be hesitant to ask in group sessions.

Sessions with administrators can be devoted to determining management philosophies of the candidates, explaining the special challenges of an advertised position, determining who among the candidates would handle situations likely to arise, and establishing their views on proposed changes within the organization. Administrators should be honest in pointing out that the organization seeks people who can tolerate ambiguity and high levels of stress. Candidates who are open to risk-taking will want to know how the organization deals with failure, since the likelihood of failed projects is high when new approaches are tried. Reassurance and examples of how the organization supports new approaches will be helpful. Candidates who like challenges will usually let interviewers know that they would like to be a part of the change effort and their energy level will rise as plans and goals are discussed. If someone is too concerned with assurances and has serious doubts, he or she is probably not the best choice for a position that will demand much flexibility, a high frustration level, and self-assurance.

Interview questions to be asked by the committee or by administrators should be carefully worded and designed to elicit information needed, sometimes without the candidate being aware that he or she is providing revealing data that will be helpful in the selection process.

Sample lists of questions for candidates for key managerial positions might include some of the following. The type of information that might be revealed in the answer to the question is indicated on some of the questions.

1. What are your present supervisor's responsibilities? (Will indicate level of responsibility the candidate has within the organization of which he or she is a part.)
2. Describe a typical day (or week) in your present position. (Indicates types of tasks the candidate spends time on and whether he or she is a crisis manager.)
3. How have you decided to hire the people you have hired in your present position? (Indicates what he or she deems important in staff.)
4. What do you consider the single most important accomplishment in your present job? In your career to date? (Indicates what is important to him or her.)
5. What do you consider to be your most important responsibilities in the position for which you are applying?
6. If you had an employee resist change, what would you do?
7. What specific strengths did you bring to your present job that made you effective?
8. What specific strengths do you think you would bring to the position for which you are applying?
9. How do you make important decisions?
10. What might you have done in your present position to be more successful?
11. What interests you in this job?
12. Describe your career goals.
13. What have been your biggest failures or frustrations?
14. What risks have you taken in your present position?
15. Describe a failure you have had and how it occurred.
16. What do you like about your present employer?
17. What do you do when you're having trouble solving a problem?
18. Describe the best boss you've ever had.

People who will be interviewing the candidates will also have access to the files being kept on each of them. Candidates and their references should be made aware that these files will be open so they know that anything they put in writing will become public information.

In the course of conducting the group interviews, employees who are unhappy with the changes taking place within the organization or who develop a dislike for a particular candidate may use the interview process to vent their anger either in how they phrase a question, the tone of their voice, or their actions during the course of the interview. If someone behaves in an unacceptable manner, he or she should first be asked by the person moderating the interview session to rephrase the question and be told why the action is not appropriate. If the employee persists in creating a disturbance, he or she should be asked to leave the interview; if he or she refuses, the moderator should end the interview session immediately. It is the responsibility of the search committee and the organization to ensure that the interview is conducted properly. If there is any indication of harassment, the opportunity for disruption should be removed by ending the session.

Reference Checks

Applicants for support positions and professional positions will supply references when submitting an application. It is up to the library to determine which or how many references to check. In addition, the candidate may be asked if he or she objects to other people being contacted.

Names identified as references are usually people the applicant knows will supply a positive reference. However, when reviewing the reference letter or phone call, the interviewer should be alert to subtle nuances or omissions that indicate potential problems.

Those checking references should also be aware that contacting individuals other than those cited as references may lead to complaints being filed by the applicant. Within the library field, it is not unusual for people to use their professional networks to obtain additional information about applicants for professional positions. This should be done with care, however, since the candidate may justifiably complain or sue the library if such information is used to deny the applicant the position.

In the search and interview process, credentials should be carefully examined for appropriateness to the position for which an applicant is applying and for accuracy. A false or misleading statement on a resume is an indication of a maladjusted approach to life, a clue to potential problems. When reviewing credentials, such as a resume, interviewers should not be swayed by inappropriate credentials; they should also be sensitive to employment patterns.

Donna Post, head of cataloging, was eager to fill the cataloging vacancy. The candidate who was being interviewed today seemed to be the best of all the ones interviewed thus far. Larry Olsen had been a librarian for 12 years and had held several cataloging positions, with different subject cataloging skills, usually changing jobs about every two years. He had gained some valuable experience that Donna thought would be helpful in the cataloging position for which he had applied. As she talked to Larry, she asked him to share with her why he had left some of the jobs. In each instance, Larry had disagreed with the person to whom he reported and had decided to move to another job. In his present position, his supervisor insisted that each cataloger's work be revised by another member of the staff, a policy that Larry found demeaning.

Donna was impressed that despite all the job changes, Larry had found time to complete the course requirements for his doctorate. For the past few years he had been researching his dissertation which he planned to finish within the next year. Donna thought his doctorate in Romance languages would be invaluable to the organization.

Donna offered Larry the job. Within one year, she found it necessary to fire him.

****

What were the clues Donna should have noted on Larry's resume?

The frequency of job changes, without noticeable advancement in responsibilities, was certainly a clue, particularly when Larry himself indicated that disagreement with his supervisor was usually a factor in the job change. Donna was also influenced by her awe for his doctorate work, a credential that was nonessential for the cataloging position though his language skills would be helpful. His slowness in completing the requirements for the degree may also be another clue, indicating lack of commitment to any chosen path.

ORIENTATION AND TRAINING OF NEW EMPLOYEES

Once the interviewing has been completed, the hiring decision has been made, and the employee is on board, the critical phase of orientation and training begins. The appropriate introduction of a new employee to a library can make easier his or her integration into the organization and contribute to years of satisfying, productive service. Orientation responsibilities are usually shared among the personnel office of a library, the hiring department, and the personnel department of the parent organization.

Library Personnel Office

The library's personnel office prepares all necessary paperwork to hire a new employee and may write a letter of welcome, stating the expected beginning date of employment and whom to report to on the first day of work. In many organizations an orientation checklist is placed in the new employee's folder and filled out as steps are completed.

The orientation responsibilities of the personnel office may include an introduction to the overall organization. Many libraries use audio-visual presentations to familiarize a new employee with the organizational structure, the major functional areas of the library, and the administrators responsible for these areas. In addition, general and specific library policies and expectations will be shared, usually by providing a staff handbook or through an orientation session. Follow-up sessions may be built in to provide the employee with an opportunity to ask additional questions after having been on the job for awhile. In some libraries, all employees get to meet the library director within the first three months of employment; the personnel department is responsible for setting up the appointment.

Parking assignments, the physical layout of the library, and procedures to follow to receive a staff identification card should all be explained during the first day of employment to enable the employee to come to work without major problems. As soon as the paperwork for a new employee is processed, his or her name should be placed on the appropriate library and organizational mailing lists.

Personnel office staff are responsible for monitoring that all orientation steps are completed.

Hiring Department

After a hiring decision is made and before the new employee arrives, the department head needs to prepare other staff members for the new employee. A work area should be prepared with necessary supplies or equipment. A current job description should be available and a training plan prepared. If staff was not involved in the hiring decision, the reasons for hiring a particular employee may be shared together with the new employee's previous work experience, education, and training. The responsibilities of the new employee may be explained to other staff members and training responsibilities assigned.

On the first day of employment, after an initial meeting with the personnel office staff, the new employee should be welcomed by his or her supervisor or the person who made the hiring decision. After being assigned a workplace, the employee should be introduced to coworkers and work relationships explained by the supervisor. A short discussion of each employee's background and interests may be helpful in order to familiarize the new person with the personal attributes of coworkers.

Next, the work of the department should be explained in more detail than took place in the interview. The supervisor should describe functions and objectives of the department, outline the organization of the department, and explain the new employee's role in the unit. Work relationships should be outlined in detail, stressing supervisory responsibilities and reporting lines.

The responsibility of showing the new employee the layout of the department and/or library may be assigned to a coworker. It will be necessary to show where restrooms, break facilities, elevators, and water fountains are located.

A brief introduction to the head of the department, if he or she is not the supervisor, may follow, with a more in-depth interview arranged for a later time (ideally within the first month after the employee begins employment).

To help the new employee get socialized, the supervisor may arrange to have a coworker take the new employee to lunch and on breaks the first day.

Part of the first day should be devoted to explaining work rules and regulations and the department's expectations concerning:

- attendance and punctuality
- breaks and lunch periods
- sick leave and vacation
- time sheets
- probationary period and evaluations
- office telephone and answering procedures
- other departmental procedures, as applicable

The new employee cannot be expected to remember all these instructions and details. A well-developed staff handbook can be assigned as required reading for the remainder of the first day. A detailed training plan should be provided and its purpose explained to the employee; the second day of employment should start with a discussion of the plan.

The Personnel Department of the Parent Organization

If the library is part of a larger organization, e.g., a university or city, the personnel department of the larger organization may also have some orientation session to explain organization benefits like retirement, insurance, and leave provisions.

Orientation

Orientation to a library can be complex and confusing, especially in a large organization and to an employee new to the library field. Having an orientation checklist, which is filed in the employee's permanent personnel file, will help lessen the confusion and ensure that all steps are covered. An example of an orientation checklist appears here.

Figure 5. Example of an Orientation Checklist

```
                        NAME OF LIBRARY
                       Orientation Checklist

Employee's Name _____

Job Title _____

Department _____ Starting Date_____

Date Orientation Completed _____


  I.   PREPARATIONS BEFORE ARRIVAL OF NEW EMPLOYEE
       (A)  Personnel Office
            (1)  Write a letter offering the position _____
            (2)  Send a letter of welcome _____
            (3)  Set entrance conference date _____
            (4)  Complete necessary paperwork for hiring employee
                 _____

       (B)  Department Head
            (1)  Inform all staff of starting date of new employee
                 _____
            (2)  Copy job description and adjust training plan
                 _____
            (3)  Prepare a workplace, including supplies and equipment
                 _____
            (4)  Place employee's name on library mailing list
                 _____

 II.   WELCOMING THE NEW EMPLOYEE
       (A)  Personnel Office
            (1)  Explain personnel policies and procedures
                 _____
            (2)  Review parking and ID procedures
                 _____
            (3)  Arrange orientation session with parent organization
                 _____

       (B)  Supervisor
            (1)  Welcome employee and explain your relationship to him/her
                 _____
            (2)  Assign a workplace, materials, supplies _____
            (3)  Introduce employee to coworkers
III.   LIBRARY TOUR
       (A)  Personnel Office
            (1)  Give general tour of the library and show the employee:
                 (a)  staff rooms _____
                 (b)  elevators _____
                 (c)  restrooms _____
                 (d)  water fountains _____
                 (e)  emergency exits _____
                 (f)  stacks _____
                 (g)  main library divisions_____
       (B)  Department
            (1)  Explain the layout of the department _____
 IV.   EXPLANATION OF THE FUNCTIONS OF THE DEPARTMENT
       (1)  Explain goals and objectives _____
       (2)  Explain organizational structure and reporting lines
            _____
```

(3)   Discuss the employee's work in relation to other positions

(4)   Schedule a session with the department head, if applicable

V.   EXPLANATION OF LIBRARY RULES AND REGULATIONS
   (A)   Personnel Office
      (1)   Working hours _____
      (2)   Punctuality and attendance _____
      (3)   Lunch and breaks _____
      (4)   Time sheets, if applicable _____
      (5)   Probationary period and evaluations _____
      (6)   Use of office equipment _____
   (B)   Supervisor
      (1)   Other relevant departmental policies _____
VI.   SCHEDULE FOLLOW UP INTERVIEWS WITH
   (A)   Personnel Office
      (1)   Schedule Interview with
         (a)   Associate/Assistant Director of libraries after 1 month
         (b)   Personnel Director after 2 months
         (c)   Library Director after 3 months
   (B)   Supervisor
      (1)   Implement training plan
VII.   COMPLETION OF EVALUATION FORM AFTER
    PROBATIONARY PERIOD _____

EMPLOYEE TRAINING

Preparing a well-organized training program for new employees will ease their integration into the organization. It will minimize their anxieties and frustrations by explaining the library's work expectations and conveying that they are important to the organization.

Ideally supervisors will provide a well-written job description *and* a training plan to each employee on the first working day. The job description will outline the scope of the position and the principle responsibilities, while the training plan will specify in what order the duties should be learned and how long it will take to master each task.

Trainers

If training is to be successful, the supervisor and/or trainer should exhibit a positive attitude, show respect for the responsibilities to be performed by the new employee, and present the training program as an active process and a valuable learning experience. Whenever possible, the previous experience of a new employee should be recognized as relevant and transferable to newly required duties.

Training responsibilities should be assigned to employees who are friendly, supportive of, and knowledgeable about the overall organizational structure and goals as well as the role their department will play in achieving these goals. Trainers should be able to relate the new employee's responsibilities to the overall mission of the library and convey how a job well done will positively affect the ability of other people to perform their duties well.

Effective trainers will also be able to explain to the new employee the subtleties of the organizational climate and what work-related behaviors will lead to success. Trainers should also be open to new ideas and suggestions that incoming employees may have. New employees view each task in an unbiased way, so they may suggest more efficient methods of performing their responsibilities. If suggestions are ignored or discouraged during the initial training period, a new employee will lose interest in making suggestions and perceive the library as a closed system, unwilling to listen to employee input. Changing organizations cannot afford to ignore anyone's suggestions in making the organization more effective.

Careless remarks by trainers about the lack of importance of a new employee's position or their perception of how boring certain tasks are will give the newly hired person the impression that his or her contribution and capabilities will be undervalued by the organization. The new employee was hopefully selected to best meet the requirements of a particular position, and if that position is not important to a library, it should have been phased out.

Training responsibilities may be shared among several people. Each trainer's areas of expertise and responsibilities need to be clearly outlined in order to overcome confusion by a new worker. Shared training will promote team building, since all persons involved will have a stake in the new employee's success. The trainee, on the other hand, will benefit from the experience of many people and gain respect for each person's competence and knowledge.

Training Plans for New Employees

To prepare a general training plan for each vacancy, a supervisor/trainer should start by listing all tasks the employee in that position must perform. The person leaving the position should ideally be enlisted to either help develop a new training plan or update an existing one.

Next, the major tasks should be identified and prioritized. Special attention needs to be paid to those tasks on which others are built; tasks that are absolutely essential to the position should be indicated.

After a candidate has been chosen for a position, the general training plan should be examined and compared with the candidate's experience. Modifications in the plan should be made, taking into consideration the new employee's knowledge, special skills, abilities, and weaknesses.

All training plans need to explain the objectives of the training and why training is necessary. They should outline which responsibilities need to be learned first, how long it should take under normal circumstances to perform them, and what constitutes inadequate, good, or excellent performance. If more than one person is involved in the training, the name of each trainer needs to be provided with the tasks for which he or she is responsible.

Besides listing the time frames for each responsibility to be learned, it will be helpful to a new employee to know how long the overall training period will last. In most organizations, the training or probationary period lasts six months, during which time an employee can be dismissed should performance not meet stated expectations. Because of this tentative work relationship, new employees need to receive continuous feedback during their training period.

Trainers should schedule periodic consultation sessions in all training plans to give employees an opportunity to ask questions and receive recognition for their successes. If problems arise, trainers can check if their instructions were clear, if policies and procedures were understood, or if the employees are unable or unwilling to learn required tasks. Sometimes trainers base their expectations on the previous performances of one outstanding individual and they establish unrealistic time frames for learning new tasks for subsequent employees. Scheduled feedback sessions can help to identify unrealistic expectations, and adjustments in the training plan can be negotiated if necessary. If work problems develop, however, the trainer needs to address them as soon as they occur and before they become habits. If they persist after being discussed, termination of an employee who is still in training may prevent more frustrating and costly solutions later. Ideally the feedback session will be used to express support and interest in an employee's progress.

Retraining

Training plans can also be developed for experienced staff with performance problems. Because performance expectations are likely to change drastically when libraries are in transition, retraining may be necessary for employees who have not kept up their professional skills or who are bored with their career and do not attend to their responsibilities. Training plans may also be used when employees are reassigned to other positions as a result of organizational restructuring or their own inadequacies. An example of a training plan is included in the appendix.

Before embarking on retraining, the organization should communicate its expectations clearly and provide opportunities for employees to update their skills voluntarily. If they prefer old habits and show an unwillingness to change, a formalized retraining program may need to be developed. As with training programs for new employees, major responsibilities will be identified and prioritized and performance expectations clearly stated. To help the employee understand why retraining is necessary, the reasons for the changes should be explained and, if necessary, other choices outlined. Understanding why there may be resistance to change may help a supervisor to constructively address it. If training does not prove successful within specified time frames, the employee will have to be either transferred or dismissed.

TERMINATION OF EMPLOYEES

Every library manager, every supervisor, will at some point in his or her career have to recommend the termination of an employee. Sometimes this will be necessary related to a downturn in the economy and the resulting budget reductions for the library. In such a situation, layoffs will result. Staff may also have to be terminated when a project being funded by grant money ends; usually personnel are aware when hired that the position ends with the completion of the project. In an academic setting, librarians may be terminated as a result of not obtaining a continuing appointment; usually personnel in such situations are aware of the results of not achieving tenure so the termination is not a surprise, though the decision may be challenged. Of greater concern to managers is termination of an employee related to inappropriate or inadequate job performance—the firing of an employee.

Firing Employees

It is never pleasant to fire an employee, no matter how disruptive an individual is, how incompatible with the organizational goals he or she proves to be, or how incompetent or untrainable he or she is. The unpleasantness is evident to the person being terminated, the person doing the terminating, and to the organization itself. Termination of an individual may be felt to have been well deserved by other employees within the organization, but there will also be individuals who feel that the termination was not warranted or was too drastic an action.

Firing, as opposed to termination for other reasons such as funding problems, generally takes place after extensive efforts have been made to improve the employee's job performance. When the firing decision is made, the supervisor realizes that the individual will be deprived of income and may have great difficulty in finding another job in a similar capacity. For an employee who is a member of the support staff, moving to another clerical job may be a possibility. But for a librarian with the appropriate professional educational credentials, firing from a position may very well make it difficult, if not impossible, to find another job of similar responsibilities in the library field.

Managers joining the staff of libraries that are in transition may find that already on board are staff who managed to function under the old guidelines of acceptable behavior or who were in positions that limited disciplinary action related to their inappropriate activities. Staff morale might have been low in the past but the organizational goals dictated that corrective action did not take place against people who functioned inadequately. The reasons may have been that the employee in question was protected by the administration with its similar problems or he or she successfully threatened legal action if discipline was to be forthcoming; often employees in libraries have benefited from an organizational philosophy that personnel problems were to be ignored. Sometimes employees might also have benefited from the fact that they functioned in an area of specialization where there was no one in a knowledgeable position to question their performance.

When an organization begins to change and establishes different standards of behavior and job performance, there will be some staff who choose to ignore the new guidelines or, because of lack of knowledge and abilities, cannot follow the revised expectations. In such a situation two avenues are likely. Such staff will either become very visible or will fade into the background. The visible employees who begin to have problems with the new expectations may attempt to capitalize on the confusion as new guidelines are put into place. They may seize additional authority or prove to be disruptive and accusatory, attacking new policies and procedures. For the employee who tries to become invisible to the administration, the problems may surface as increasingly inadequate work performance, confusion over expectations, and withdrawal from organizational activities.

Jerri Angellini had been hired shortly after Ethel Matteson became head of the prepping area. Jerri appeared to have the typing and dexterity skills that were needed to label and prep library materials and to enter the data into the online system. She seemed to respond to initial training and perform adequately.

After a couple of weeks, the shelvers began to bring back book trucks of errors in labels; the circulation staff began to note inputting mistakes. Ethel traced the errors to Jerri and talked to her, showing her examples of the errors and explaining the problems that ensued. Jerri improved for a few days, then errors began to be noticed again. When Ethel discussed the errors with Jerri, Jerri insisted she was being singled out because she was new to the organization and was an older woman. Ethel patiently explained that her newness to the organization and her age were irrelevant and that she should correct her work habits. The next day Jerri was late to work. When she came in, she gave Ethel and Ethel's supervisor a lengthy written tirade, charging discrimination.

Ethel continued to work with Jerri, and after each concentrated training session, there would be some improvement. However, when Jerri was left on her own, she reverted to sloppy work patterns with a high error rate; she also told other employees that she was being put under unreasonable pressure and was a target of age discrimination.

After three months, Ethel and her supervisor decided that continued efforts to train Jerri to be a valuable addition to the staff were fruitless; they gathered their documentation of poor work and the reports they had written after each session with Jerri in which she had been apprised of her inadequate work. In a brief session with Jerri, they informed her that she would be terminated. Jerri stormed out of the office, slamming the door. She went to the personnel relations officer and charged age discrimination. In the investigation that followed, the personnel relations officer reviewed the examples of Jerri's work, the efforts made to help her improve, and ruled that there was no discrimination involved.

****

Do you believe that Ethel was justified in firing Jerri? Was Jerri capable of performing her job? What steps did Ethel take to convey performance expectations? Were they sufficient?

The library had done its best to make Jerri a contributing member of the organization. When the managers observed a pattern in Jerri's behavior and her resistance to complying with work standards, they began to keep examples of her errors and to document their sessions with her. When the age discrimination charges were levied against the library, the personnel relations officer could see in his review that the organization was not at fault, the employee was.

Administrators in a transitional organization often are individuals who have been brought in from outside the structure and who are expected to make changes that lead to a better, more effective organization. One of their first responsibilities should be to assess the strengths and weaknesses of the existing staff. This will mean long hours devoted to analyzing past work practices and identifying the individuals who are willing and able to move forward with the changing expectations. To give each employee a chance to become a part of an emerging institution, changing organizations should try to clearly communicate their expectations, identify staff deficiencies, seek ways to strengthen staff performance and make it possible for staff to participate in forging the new directions of the organization, establish time frames for necessary improvements, analyze and change organizational constraints that hinder adequate performance, and reassign individuals when appropriate.

Staff encountering difficulty in making the transition to new expectations may need continuing education to improve performance, may need to seek counseling to cope with changed expectations, or may need to be moved into a position where they can adequately function within the organization. Supervisors observing such employees should communicate their expectations, relay their observations, assist the individual in the transition, and be poised to suggest a reassignment if the organizational expectations cannot be realized within the individual's present position. It should be stated clearly that unsatisfactory performance in a position will not be acceptable but that the organization will do what it can to assist the employee in improvement of performance within a reasonable time frame.

Peggy Petes had worked in Interlibrary Loan for many years and had developed an extensive knowledge of the collections in all the libraries in the system. However, she disliked the new interlibrary loan procedures adopted by the consortium and had resisted the use of automation. When a new system director, Granville Marshall, was hired, he tried to start a new mechanism for selection of materials for the main library and the branches. He wanted the reference staff to participate more in the selection process; the reference staff was resistant. The acquisitions staff, which had been responsible for much of the selection, welcomed the transfer of responsibilities that had become virtually unmanageable as the system grew in size.

The new director analyzed the talents of the staff. He observed that Peggy had broad knowledge of the system's collections and was highly respected by other staff but that she was frustrated by the new interlibrary loan system. He asked her to work with the acquisitions staff to learn more about the selection process; the acquisitions staff prepared a step-by-step training program for Peggy. After several months of training, the director reassigned Peggy to the reference staff to train them in selection techniques. A reference librarian who had once voiced an interest in interlibrary loan and who needed more predictable hours for family reasons was in turn trained by Peggy to do interlibrary loan.

Peggy encountered some resistance but, after several months, the reference staff began to select materials with enthusiasm. Peggy coordinated the efforts with the needs of the acquisitions department and a successful collection development program was the result.

****

The new director observed a need, identified an individual who had the skills to fill that need, and by putting the right people in the right place, challenged existing staff to meet changing expectations.

What if the results had been different and Peggy had proved resistant to changing responsibilities? What if she had disliked being given different job assignments and had resented being retrained after a lengthy period in a particular position?

When all attempts for performance improvement fail and the employee does not reach an acceptable performance level, the individual should be terminated. If the individual simply did not have the abilities to improve and reach the organization's performance levels, the organization may be able to assist with or advise the person on future career plans. If, however, the employee adamantly refused to change his or her expectations and job performance and proved insubordinate and perhaps even disruptive, the organization should divorce itself from the employee since further contact will only increase the former employee's frustration level. An employee, with an uncooperative attitude that precludes improvement and promotes disruption can only continue to be a hindrance to organizational progress.

It is one thing for an employee to fail because of inabilities and quite another for the individual to not only fail because of inabilities but also to prove insubordinate or disruptive when the organization attempts to help the individual improve. Changing organizations will most likely resolve both problems.

Supervisors should document the steps taken to assist all employees in working within the transitional organization. Discussions with such individuals should be summarized in writing with copies sent to the employee. Incidents that are observed should be documented. Goals should be identified and discussed with the employee, with the expectations and methodology for reaching those goals as well as the time frame spelled out in writing.

As Peggy succeeded in her new job, the director was pleased to have had a successful transfer of a long-term employee. He had, however, also observed that the head of cataloging, Ernest Danvers, was performing inadequately, preferring to perform clerical tasks and refusing to streamline the procedures as automation increasingly became a part of the library's operation. Ernest tried to undermine all efforts to revise his procedures and openly countermanded the director's requests for procedural changes. He told other staff that the director was just an upstart who didn't know anything about cataloging. The director, after several months, began to consider transferring Ernest and appointing a new head of cataloging. He observed in Ernest's file that he had once worked in reference. The director decided to transfer Ernest to reference and asked the head of reference to draft a training plan.

Ernest was angry about the transfer and his loss of a managerial position, though he had been performing inadequately. He began talking to librarians elsewhere in the library system about the director's alleged incompetence. That became Ernest's chief topic of conversation at coffee and over lunch. The other librarians, noting the director's ability to initiate new programs, his success in redirecting Peggy's skills, and the positive results of changes in several policies and procedures, discounted Ernest's statements. As he became more and more disruptive, both in his interactions with other staff and his work with patrons, it was obvious something had to be done. The head of reference had numerous discussions with Ernest about his behavior. Ernest always disagreed with her, even when documentation was presented. The reference head documented the conversations, sending a copy to the director as well as to Ernest. After several months, it was clear that Ernest had no intention of being retrained to his new position and he was terminated.

****

How do you think the staff responded to Ernest's termination? Do you believe termination of professional librarians is necessary under certain circumstances? Can you give some examples?

Although these efforts are time-consuming, if all efforts to retrain or correct the performance of the employee fail and termination is necessary, these documentations will support the final, necessary decision. The steps taken will indicate good faith on the part of the organization and the supervisors to aid the employee in making the transition. If the employee tried but could not reach the expectation levels, these documented efforts will also prove valuable in identifying possibilities for future training or career paths since the documentation will show the areas where the individual cannot function at an acceptable level.

If the employee was unwilling to change and fought efforts made to assist him or her, the documentation will provide justification for firing. In either situation, the documentation is valuable if a grievance is filed or other action is taken as recourse against the termination step.

Public sector or regulated organizations will probably have operating procedures and guidelines established that spell out the steps to take when final disciplinary action is deemed necessary. Supervisors who identify an employee who is a potential problem should involve personnel officers, counselors, or other experienced individuals. They can serve as resource people, and in some instances, witness disciplinary conversations.

Operating in a vacuum in a disciplinary matter is likely to fly back into the face of the supervisor who chose to pursue the matter alone, without other advice or guidance. Those consultants already on staff can advise when the discipline is too severe or is inappropriate, can confirm the actions and words of the supervisor engaged in disciplinary action, and can reinforce supervisory action by explaining to the employee that he or she is being disciplined in a reasonable manner. While the consultant can serve as a witness and advisor, he or she may also find him or herself the target of abuse from the upset employee. Thus, a part of the role of advisor or consultant is to be ready to accept that the anger and repercussions may also have a negative, uncomfortable, and potentially long-term connotation for the disciplinarian.

It is critical not to be too hasty in firing an employee. The employee should be given the opportunity and guidance to become an integral part of the new organization. If it is necessary to terminate that employee, it will be evident to all employees that the organization provided the individual with the opportunity to become a functioning part of the changing organization. While the evaluation of the employee's abilities and role within the organization is undergoing analysis and the termination decision is being made, other employees will be assessing the organization's efforts to help that individual. If all proper steps have been followed and assistance was offered to an individual, it will have become clear to the rest of the organization that the employee's position and actions were untenable and the organization had no option other than terminating the employee for cause.

When contemplating termination of an employee, the supervisor should always consult the parent organization's personnel office concerning interpretation of personnel termination procedure. Legal counsel and the affirmative action officer should be involved before action is taken. This will ensure that due process has been followed, that appropriate notice is given, and that progressive disciplinary options have been used prior to the termination. Not only will checking with these individuals protect supervisors from acting hastily, but these individuals will appreciate being apprised of the action about to take place so they are aware of the background and can appropriately respond to the filing of grievances or other protests of the termination.

In summary, in an organization in transition, strengths and weaknesses of staff should be identified early in the transitional stage. Assistance should be given to staff having adjustment problems, including counseling, setting of goals, and timeframes. When an employee cannot cope with the changes taking place, termination may be necessary. This may happen because the employee really cannot attain adequate job performance or because the employee is resistant to change.

Chapter 8
Effective Staff Use in a Changing Library

STAFFING LEVELS AND REASSIGNMENT OF RESPONSIBILITIES

Appropriate and effective usage of an organization's human resources is critical, especially within a library undergoing transition. Poor use of staff can ultimately destroy an organization. Managers in libraries in transition must be particularly cognizant of the available human resources and rely on them to bring about changes that need to take place.

As the new organization evolves, new expectations and processes for attaining those expectations should be introduced. Staffing arrangements must be examined. As service, policies, and procedures change, some areas of the library will be found to have too much staff while others will seem to have too little staff. Other staffing problems may be a result of inappropriate staffing ratios such as too many librarians and too few support staff.

As responsibilities shift and work processes change, staffing levels and assignments must be continuously examined to adapt the organization to its new functions and direction. For example, the introduction of automation may result in the need for more managers, fewer librarians involved in the operational aspect, and more support staff. Professional staff may be shifted to managerial positions or to parts of the organization where their skills can be better used, such as in reference or instructional positions. The ratio of professionals to support staff will change, with professionals decreasing in some areas and increasing in others.

Reassigning staff can prove threatening to those being reassigned and uncomfortable to those doing the reassigning. Staff may be reassigned because the direction of the organization has changed and their skills are no longer appropriate for their area of the organization, they have proven unqualified for the position formerly held, or they are in constant conflict with coworkers. If the employee has certain needed skills, an effort may be made to find a position he or she can fill with those skills and in consideration of their present mental frame of mind.

It is important that staff be open about suggesting changes and that they feel they can come forward and suggest potential reassignments. What is critical is that the staff not be allowed or encouraged to suggest reassignments for reasons of revenge against employees with whom they have feelings of resentment. Staff should be encouraged to suggest possible reorganizations or reassignments for the good of the library; these changes should contribute to the accomplishment of the mission of the library.

Reassignment can be an effective way to deal with shifting staffing patterns or with dysfunctional staff. On the other hand, reassigning staff has been overused in the past as a way to dump nonfunctional staff on another area of the organization. Thus, care should be taken when contemplating reassignment to analyze why the reassigning is being considered and what problems it is to alleviate.

Is it because the staffing needs have shifted? If that is the situation, where will the skills of the employees to be shifted best be utilized? Are staff being shifted because they aren't functioning in their present assignments? If so, will they be able to function in their new assignments or are they being set up to fail once again? Can training be provided to help them reach acceptable performance levels?

If, however, reassignment is being used as a way to simply get rid of unsatisfactory employees with whom the former supervisor is unwilling to continue to cope, reconsideration of reassignment should take place. An employee who has repeatedly proven inadequate or difficult, for whatever reason, should not be put into a no-win position by being dumped on some other part of the organization. Instead, the employee's inadequacies and problems should be analyzed and addressed. Indeed, the problems may be that adequate supervision has been missing and the employee has been an unwitting victim.

Within too many libraries, a particular department or area has been unofficially designated as the organizational dumping ground. As a result that department internalizes feelings of inadequacy or victimization and eventually becomes inoperative. We all know examples where individuals with personality or interaction problems were transferred to a processing department such as cataloging or acquisitions. Other examples might be the assignment of unorganized people who lack management skills to positions limited to nonpeak reference service.

Prior to reassignment of staff, the reason for reassignment should be explained. If it is because of changing organizational needs and the fact that overstaffing exists in some areas, the reassigned individual should be told that is the reason and that, if attrition takes place in the overstaffed area, he or she can apply for a transfer back if desired. No guarantees should be given, however.

If, on the other hand, reassignment is taking place because of consistent inadequate job performance or the absence of skills appropriate to the former position, the employee should be told this, too, so he or she will know what skills are lacking. It is unfair to tell an employee that reassignment is taking place without informing him or her of the reason.

Staff being reassigned because of overstaffing in an area may choose to seek employment elsewhere; in this case, the organization should provide assistance. Staff being reassigned because of their own inadequacies may also seek employment elsewhere and, by being told of their shortcomings, can seek positions in different career paths rather than repeating the mistakes they have already made in job choices. Employers may elect to suggest a deadline before which employees reassigned due to performance inadequacies will need to locate another position in another organization or make a career change.

Reassigning of employees may also be the result of a consolidation of activities, such as the coordination of management of two automated systems under one automation coordinator position. The trend of merging or integrating technical and public service activities may result in one senior-level administrator rather than two or three. As a result of such a merger of activities, individuals who were functioning in line positions may find themselves reassigned to other positions. Usually this happens as positions become vacant, but it may also be the result of performance problems which must be addressed.

Sometimes staff positions are created to facilitate organizational development and communication. These staff positions should be used to the fullest extent to free line administrators from routine or important but time-consuming tasks, such as maintenance of physical facilities, development work, personnel and continuing education activities, and special projects. This is not to imply that all staff positions are created to provide employment for individuals who have not functioned adequately in line positions. However, staff positions are often structured to fit the particular talents of persons who have been in positions where they could no longer meet the needs and expectations of the organization.

There should be concrete reasons for reassignment or organizational restructuring. The reassignment, especially if it leads to organizational restructuring, should be a decision that originates among the staff involved, perhaps as a suggestion, before it is implemented by the chief administrator.

Libraries should capitalize on opportunities to examine organizational structure. A critical time for reexamination of a library hierarchy or departmental interrelationships is when a valuable employee resigns or retires or an unsuitable individual departs the organization. When this opportunity presents itself, the managers should discuss possible restructuring of the organization or at least review potential redesigning of the vacant position. This should result from consultation with other staff, including discussions with individuals who may vocally disagree with the changes. Such individuals can contribute insight into particular problems that may arise and they also need to have the opportunity to voice their disagreement prior to any reorganization taking place.

In some libraries chief administrators who elect to step down—or are forced to step down—often want to continue to contribute to the organization but find themselves unwanted or in an awkward situation. Will the organization be willing to retain them in a nondecision-making role? Will their presence be viewed as nonthreatening? If they elect to move to another library, but in a subordinate role, will they be viewed as failures in their former position? It is unfortunate, but true, that the library profession has not determined how to effectively use former senior administrators when these individuals decide they have had enough of the responsibilities of senior management but still want to practice their library skills both to help the library and to continue to earn a living.

In some parent organizations a role outside the library may be found for these senior administrators, working on projects or providing staff administrative needs for the central administrative unit. In other organizations, the individuals will be retained within the library but will be assigned to responsibilities such as fund raising, management of special collections, or administration of a small, perhaps inconspicuous unit within the library.

If the reassignment of the senior administrator is due to inadequate job performance, the staff will often continue to be critical of the individual's job performance and productivity. Or the staff may suddenly find itself in a secure enough position to be critical of the former administrator. If the individual sought the reassignment and has retained the respect of the staff, he or she may be viewed as a valuable advisor by the new administrator—or may be viewed as a potential power threat. Indeed, if the new administrator proves to be inadequate, the former administrator may be drafted to step in.

There are also instances where retired senior administrators who are respected by colleagues are called back into service in other libraries to serve as the chief executive officer while a search for the permanent director takes place. Usually, this takes place in libraries where the former director has been summarily dismissed, there is an unexpected and unplanned vacancy, or there are potentially sensitive personnel situations that may arise and the parent institution chooses to bring in a capable outsider to fill in and who may be able to resolve some problems while a search is in progress.

In libraries in transition, when the organizational climate is undergoing dramatic change, for example, from authoritarian to participatory management, the presence of a former senior administrator, especially one who functioned in a style opposite to the one being introduced, can be detrimental. The former administrator will likely be consulted by present employees who are having serious problems adjusting to the changes. They will come to seek advice in resisting the changes being introduced. The former administrator may assume the role of the cheerleader for dissension in such situations, so methods will have to be identified to short-circuit that role. However, these efforts to perpetuate the past will also help the new administrators to identify the change resisters so they can be counseled to become a part of the new organizational style.

In libraries where the former administrators are still present and are providing support to the change resisters, the new administrative group will usually find that the former chief administrator was the only decision maker and had a parental style of administration. The change resisters are uncomfortable with the responsibilities placed upon them by the new administration and they seek advice in evading these responsibilities by consulting the authority figure with whom they were more comfortable.

In the past organizations could force administrators to retire at a specific age, usually 65, and encourage other employees to retire completely at 70. The staff, frustrated by the individual, could at least count on the employee or administrator leaving the organization at a certain age. With the changing of the retirement laws, and the increasing concern about age discrimination, this is no longer true. Many people continue to be valuable employees into their senior years. Others, either through poor health or because of inadequate job performance, may become problem employees and if the employee is also in his or her senior years, age will be seen as the culprit. Age discrimination may be charged.

It is the responsibility of the organization to develop performance guidelines for all employees and explain expectations. If dysfunctional older employees cannot meet those expectations, rather than expecting advancing age, illness, and other factors to resolve the problems, the issues have to be addressed and documented by library managers.

EVALUATIONS

Libraries in transition have the opportunity to develop a process of evaluations that can be an effective performance management tool, fostering honest communication between managers and employees, developing continuous opportunities for feedback, providing reasons for appropriate continuing education, creating support of the organization by employees, and fostering improved performance while supporting employee growth and development.

There are several aspects of the evaluation process to consider. First, what type of evaluations will be conducted? Will these be based on completion of objectives or goals? Second, who will be evaluated? Will the evaluations be by supervisors of subordinates? Will there also be evaluations of supervisors by subordinates? Will there be peer review?

Third, how often will the evaluations take place and will they be retained in personnel files for future reference? Fourth, what format will the evaluation instrument follow? Will it be a rating system or an essay format evaluation or a combination of both? Will it be signed by both the rater and the person being evaluated? If subordinates are evaluating supervisors, will the individual comments be anonymous with a compilation of the ratings being forwarded to the person being evaluated or will the evaluations be shared with the supervisor? Note: The format decison for the evaluation should be made *after* points 1, 2, and 3 have been decided.

Fifth, will the evaluation be shared with the person being evaluated in a performance appraisal interview? Will there be the opportunity for follow-up if the need for improvement is stressed in the evaluation? Sixth, does the person being evaluated have any recourse if he or she disagrees with the evaluation?

Types of Evaluations

Let's first discuss the types of evaluations that can be conducted. Evaluations can be objective measurements of job performance, using production figures (such as in cataloging), the numbers of absences, and other gauges of performance and reliability. Thus, objective evaluations are a measurement or evaluation of the outcome of behavior, not a gauge of actual job effectiveness, an evaluation of performance. In addition, in libraries there are relatively few areas where production can be measured in a meaningful way. If employees have been evaluated on the basis of productivity, a change to a subjective evaluation process may be traumatic.

More useful to the organization are those evaluations based on subjective measures, even though these are dependent upon individual judgment. Subjective evaluations can be based on employee comparisons, (one employee's performance is compared to the performance of another in a like or similar position). The disadvantage to this type of subjective evaluation is that if one employee is particularly outstanding, other employees cannot hope to achieve those standards of performance and thus fall short in the evaluation.

Other subjective evaluations are based on rating an employee without reference to another, judging his or her performance based on his or her own abilities. Such evaluations can take the form of essays in which an individual's strengths, weaknesses, potential for further development, and constructive suggestions for improvement are described.

Another type of evaluation has the evaluator rate the individual on a behavioral performance checklist, using ratings such as poor, good, excellent, superior; poor, average, above average, exceptional; and unacceptable, needs improvement, meets position requirements, exceeds position requirements, excels in job performance. The different rating systems available are too numerous to describe in detail here. Library administrators should, however, be aware of the different types of evaluation instruments and that they can be designed to accommodate virtually every work situation.

The most effective performance evaluations probably combine a rating system that gauges the level of performance, coupled with the opportunity to make specific statements about an individual's performance, usually in essay form. Such evaluations provide positive feedback, as well as the opportunity to critique an individual on his or her outstanding attributes and suggest ways for performance improvement.

Evaluation Considerations

Who Gets Evaluated?

Who gets evaluated is the next consideration. Evaluations are most often thought of in terms of supervisors rating subordinates on job performance. Of increasing appeal are evaluations of peers and of supervisors by subordinates. In all these situations, the raters play the role of information processor, viewing the person being evaluated from vastly differing viewpoints.

Evaluations of supervisors by subordinates may be used as tools to change organizational structure if a supervisor is repeatedly evaluated negatively by subordinates. Peer evaluations can be used in a similar manner. The most effective supervisors—those who are willing to have open communication with others—will not fear subordinate or peer evaluations. On the other hand, those who realize that their performance is not effective within a particular organization and who dread honest appraisals of their performance will suffer from anxiety when subordinate or peer evaluations are contemplated.

The most common evaluations are of subordinates by supervisors. These routinely take place and are gauges of job performance by an individual in a specific position. These evaluations can be used as a basis for promotion or raises, can be tools for encouraging job performance, or can serve as disciplinary mechanisms if job performance has been unsatisfactory or improvement is needed. If a rater routinely gives glowing performance evaluations to everyone, the value of them is diminished. Similarly, if evaluations are always harsh, they will be viewed as occasions for vindictiveness and will be approached with anxiety.

Evaluation Frequency

When designing evaluation systems, the frequency should be determined and made clear to those being evaluated. Also, whether or not the resulting form will be retained in personnel files should be stated to all concerned. Nothing should ever be placed in an individual's official personnel file without the knowledge of the individual, of course.

Evaluation Format

The evaluation instrument is designed based on the type of evaluation desired, that is an objective or subjective evaluation. Many library organizations have predetermined forms, dictated by the institution of which they are a part and determined by the type of employee being evaluated. Evaluation forms for support staff tend to be based on ratings systems that rate performance levels and abilities. Evaluations for professionals tend to be more narrative in form, providing the opportunity to describe effective or ineffective job performance in essay form.

Who Sees the Evaluation?

When a supervisor is evaluating a subordinate, the use of a face-to-face performance appraisal interview is important since it provides an opportunity for both individuals to verbalize their concerns, relay positive feedback, and question performance improvement needs. In peer or upward evaluations, the appraisal interview is seldom used, probably in anticipation of the possibility of retribution if the appraisal is not positive in tone.

Possible Recourse

When an evaluation is performed, the person being evaluated should understand what recourse he or she has if he or she disagrees with the interpretations stated in the evaluation process. The options that can be exercised should be available to all employees, with the process for filing a grievance being detailed in an readily available publication.

Effective Evaluations

Increasingly, organizations are moving toward goal-setting, performance results-based evaluations whereby employees, especially professionals, can be evaluated on effectiveness and competency is based on performance in a position. Such approaches to evaluation make the appraisal process a valuable tool in human resource management rather than a required exercise.

By having a subordinate identify his or her goals for a set period of time and then performing the evaluation based on effective job performance toward reaching the stated goals, management is helping the employee to grow both personally and within the organization. Another benefit of such an approach to evaluation is that the process assists management in identifying continuing education needs, formalizing selection criteria, providing a basis for salary and promotion decisions, and isolating potential problem employees and earmarking them for additional training, counseling, or disciplinary action.

An effective evaluation system takes time, both in designing and implementing it and in using it for more effective management of human resources.

In establishing a goal-based evaluation system, care should be taken to have employees identify realistic, attainable goals that will result in improved performance for themselves and for the organization. The evaluation rating system should receive just as careful attention. Employees should understand that a rating of "unacceptable" or "needs improvement" will be taken seriously and that the employee will be provided with guidance in correcting job performance.

At the same time, employees should understand that a rating of "meets position expectations" is an acceptable rating and does not indicate mediocre performance. Most employees should strive to meet that rating level. Only the unusual or exceptional employee will attain ratings of "exceeds position requirements" or "excels" in job performance. Individuals receiving the upper ratings are probably the leaders in the organization, those who are followed by the rest of the employees and who are the initiators, the motivators—valuable employees to have on board.

If an employee receives a poor evaluation, follow-up evaluations should occur on a more frequent basis. These should be coupled with assistance from the supervisor and the organization in improving job performance. An employee who is functioning poorly or marginally should not be left to fend for him or herself. Rather than being allowed to flounder, the individual should be provided with additional training, guidance, and constructive comments in order to improve performance on the job or behavior.

An effective evaluation system can prove invaluable to a library. It can be a morale builder as employees observe an effective evaluation process reward the performers and assist the nonperformers toward improvement or disciplines them. An ineffective evaluation system has the potential of undermining morale, becoming a joke, being used as a club by management, or becoming simply a routine, bureaucratic exercise, resulting in no action or reward.

How an evaluation system is implemented is also critical. The forms should be familiar to the raters and the employees being evaluated. The rating criteria should be explained, with the individuals being rated having the opportunity to ask questions. It should be made clear that a rating such as "meets position requirements" or "acceptable performance" is a valid, positive rating and not a negative one. Those being rated should understand what action will be taken if a poor evaluation is given; that is, what assistance will be provided by the organization and the supervisor to enable the employee to improve. Raters and those being rated should also recognize that evaluations are for a specific time period, such as for a year, and are not cumulative. Thus, individuals who have performed adequately in previous years but who now are dysfunctional will find that their evaluation addresses the most recent time period. People who have functioned adequately under a previous administration and who are resistant to change will be evaluated on the basis of their present performance.

Conducting the Evaluation Interview

The evaluation interview should be undertaken in confidential, quiet surroundings so that the rater can fairly and accurately complete the form. After the evaluation is written, another individual, either an administrator at another level or a personnel officer for the organization, should review the ratings and comments made to ensure that equal and fair use of the evaluation system is being made and that one rater is not using the evaluations to discriminate against some employees while another is being too generous in rating the subordinates. This administrative review process is critical, especially in organizations with many employees and supervisors. The review makes the evaluation process more objective and omits the influence of personality in the evaluation process.

After administrative review takes place, the rater should schedule an appraisal interview with the employee. The interview should be conducted in private, in an environment conducive to discussion of the evaluation being conducted. Frank communication is essential, especially when constructive criticism is being related or there is discussion of unacceptable or marginal performance.

After the appraisal interview, the employee needing additional assistance should have the opportunity to discuss the evaluation with another person within the organization, such as a personnel officer, and should be provided with guidance in correcting any identified problems.

Finally, there should be follow-up for those individuals needing corrective assistance so that they know if they have improved or not. In some cases, where an employee has skills needed within the organization but is not functioning effectively in his or her present position, job transfer or job redesign may be a solution to the situation.

If a library has never had an effective evaluation system, the introduction of one will be traumatic to many, especially those who fear the ratings they will receive or who are uncomfortable in evaluating colleagues. Others will set unnaturally high expectations for themselves and will be demoralized when the rater doesn't share the expectation level. Others will find it difficult or impossible to accept constructive criticism and will refuse to recognize that improvement is needed. This will be especially true if the employee has been part of the library organization for many years.

A new evaluation system, or a more effective approach to an existing process, will be particularly difficult if the library is in transition, with expectations changing as the new administrators approach issues and examine policies and procedures. In a library where professionals were previously identified by their salary and educational levels, rather than by professional activities and job performance, the expectation that they be current on issues in the field and that they be willing to work to complete an assignment or project rather than adhering to a strict, tabulated work week will be difficult to change and will be traumatic to many.

Support and understanding for staff should be provided during the transition period. It will be helpful if the first round of evaluations are taken exceptionally slowly and are not considered "official." This will help employees revise their expectations, reach a clearer understanding of where the organization is headed, and accept the evaluation process and its intent.

Training sessions should be conducted during this period to teach evaluators proper techniques to use. Administrators can also use this period to identify those individuals who will attempt to use the evaluation process to intimidate employees or to improperly reward favorites. Those individuals needing guidance can also be provided with additional assistance in accepting or conducting the evaluation process. Examples of evaluation forms are included in the appendix.

GRIEVANCES

Libraries in transition will experience an increase in employee grievances until new organizational norms and expectations are established. The first grievance filed may come as a shock to a new administrator who thought changes were progressing nicely. It is important to stay calm and objective, since the grievance process itself can be used as an educational device to clarify organizational goals and expectations.

Library administrators against whom the grievances are filed need to inform themselves about the institutional grievance procedure and seek advice from all available resources, e.g., the library's personnel officer, the institutional personnel department, legal counsel, and affirmative action officer to minimize hasty conclusions or actions. If the grievance process is handled in a professional, detached manner, no matter what the outcome, employees will gain respect for the administrators trying to bring about changes. If initial grievances are resolved in favor of the new administration, other challenges to the change efforts will be minimized. If the grievances were justified, a gracious acceptance of the decision is crucial. Since grievance resolutions involve not only library staff but also parts of the parent organizations, the process can be used by managers to build credibility for themselves and their new programs. The library staff itself will be watching the process intently and managers must act calm, confident, and caring in an atmosphere that can easily become emotionally charged. Frequent interactions with staff who filed the grievance and high visibility with all staff members can reassure the organizations that grievances are not to be feared, that the managers may actually welcome the challenge as an opportunity to present the facts.

Grievances are usually time consuming and frustrating to all parties involved, but they can also be used for reexamining goals, objectives, and means. As fevers rid the body of illnesses, grievances can eradicate rumors, assumptions, misinterpretations, and misconceptions, and if handled properly, they will consolidate organizational support.

THE ROLE OF PERSONNEL OFFICERS IN MANAGING HUMAN RESOURCES

Librarians and library workers today spend most of their time managing people. As libraries have increased in complexity and personnel-related laws have multiplied, personnel issues have appeared to surface more frequently. This trend is fueled by a general lack of training of librarians in human resource management. The accelerated pace of change created by automation and technology is demanding alternative staffing patterns, job analysis, and continuing education efforts.

In addition, people working in rapidly changing environments experience high levels of stress and have an increased need for information, clarification of job expectations, reassurance of continuing worth to the organization, and communication. Library personnel officer positions are being created to meet these needs. Libraries in transition will find the personnel officer a particularly important team player in effecting change within the organization.

The principle duties of personnel officers are:

- The recruitment, orientation, and training of all levels of staff
- The establishment of classification systems, career ladders, and recommendations for salary levels
- The analysis of work flow issues and staffing needs
- The monitoring and implementation of affirmative action and equal employment opportunity programs
- The interpretation of personnel policies
- The resolution of complaints and grievances
- The negotiation of labor contracts
- The development and administration of evaluation systems
- The planning and organizing of staff development activities

- The creation and maintenance of personnel records systems
- The counseling of staff on work-related matters and referral to other agencies when needed
- The facilitating of organizational communication
- The monitoring and analyzing of personnel expenditures
- Communication with personnel units of the parent organization.

The effectiveness of personnel specialists will be dependent on their place within the organizational hierarchy and the willingness of supervisors to use their expertise. The more closely the personnel officer works with the library director and senior administrators, the more important the position will be perceived by the staff and the parent organization and the more easily it will be accepted.

To correctly analyze staffing needs, an overall perspective of a library is necessary. Personnel specialists need to be able to communicate well with professional as well as support staff and other specialists. Although in-depth knowledge of each position is not necessary, understanding the major functions and goals of departments and divisions is essential.

Confident supervisors and administrators will perceive the addition of a personnel specialist into an organization as a welcome and much needed resource. He or she will enable them to perform their supervisory functions better by providing an objective perspective on personnel-related problems, necessary legal information, possible alternatives to solve the problems, and an additional avenue of communication with employees. Arrangements for necessary continuing education seminars and training of employees will be facilitated and the overall perspective of such a specialist will help to break down territorial barriers.

Supervisors and administrators who are less secure may feel threatened by the presence of personnel specialists, resenting their "interference" in line decision-making processes. Roles may have to be clarified over an extended period of time when a personnel officer is first introduced into an organization.

Staff members in organizational units with long standing problems will see the arrival of a personnel officer as a quick solution to those problems. The administrators, on the other hand, will try to get support for their own actions from the personnel officer.

Both sides, most likely impatient because of long impasses, can grow disenchanted and disillusioned with a personnel officer when the responsibility for the problems and their resolution is placed back on their own shoulders. Opening up channels of communications, mediating between parties, and reinterpreting statements which led to misunderstandings may be all a personnel officer can do initially.

As awareness of the organizational history grows, new solutions to old problems can be tried, teaching both sides effective negotiation and communication skills. Many times when long-standing problems are examined in an unbiased and objective way, solutions become apparent or those responsible for creating and perpetuating the problems will leave. As new behaviors by remaining employees are encouraged and reinforced and as new employees are hired to replace those who left the problem situation, dynamics of interacting and communicating will change. Coworkers, instead of blaming each other, can once again start to recognize their interdependence and appreciate each other's efforts.

Personnel officers can certainly be a catalyst in bringing problems to the surface and thereby forcing them to be addressed, but the solutions usually have to be worked out between the employees who initially created the problems or have continued to foster them.

Libraries in transition have particular needs which a human resource specialist can ameliorate. Since libraries have traditionally been very structured, the uncertainties created by change will cause high levels of anxiety in many employees. Many librarians have chosen their profession because it appeared to provide a calm, undemanding, secure work environment, where the pace of work was largely under their control and goals undefinable.

Even today most people unfamiliar with library occupations envision them to be boring, stress-free, intellectually unchallenging, and dull. Occupational counselors still recommend librarianship as a profession to intelligent, but shy students who love to read. These are, of course, exceptions. Many student workers in libraries come to love and enjoy the special challenges they unexpectedly find in their work and decide to pursue librarianship as a career. Others love to open the universe of knowledge to the curious by teaching them library and research skills, while many come to enjoy the satisfaction of developing and managing professionals and a highly educated support staff.

To motivate the various personality types through a successful change effort requires vision, excellent human relation skills, and patience. A good personnel officer can assist in the development of all of the above. If he or she is part of the top administrative team, he or she will be involved in long-range planning efforts and know where the organization is moving and whether the necessary human resources and skills are already present. The personnel officer can help translate the vision into reality by identifying in-house staff with the necessary skills or the ability to develop them or by hiring new staff with the necessary qualifications. Continuing education seminars can be developed to establish future goals, to discuss the evolving organization, to provide opportunities to acquire missing expertise, and to develop human relations skills.

Supervisors and administrators solving the problems of implementing change often become frustrated when dealing with change resisters. The perspective of someone outside the situation can keep them from making decisions based on the frustrations of the moment, considering long-term consequences and gains.

In most change efforts resulting from technological innovation, the fear of losing one's job is a major concern to many employees, especially older ones who may question their own ability to upgrade or change skills levels. They need to be reassured that their skills are valuable and needed in the newly emerging library and that the organization will invest time and resources to allow them to acquire the skills necessary to succeed.

Creating a personnel specialist position with responsibilities for staff development will give employees the message that the library is serious about and willing to commit resources to foster their skills development. For those employees who are unwilling or unable to change, library personnel officers can provide career guidance and referrals to agencies which are better able to help with the severe stresses caused by displacement.

Most employees, when appropriately motivated, will rise to the challenges offered by change and experience a new growth period in their professional lives. Personnel officers can help to clarify the new organizational expectations, reinforce the arguments that the changes are positive for both employees and the library, and provide the necessary continuing education to facilitate the transitional period.

In any organization undergoing major changes, conflict heightens. Employees not only disagree about the need for changes but also disagree about how fast the changes should be implemented, who will benefit, and who will lose. Initially, administrators often will see a resurgence of territorialism. If change efforts progress well in one area of the organization and are slow in others, the dissatisfaction of employees wanting the changes will increase and frustration with those holding back may cause serious work flow problems.

Personnel officers can also be helpful in absorbing the emotional reactions to change from employees. They can help relieve staff of the initial frustration by carefully listening and reassuring all sides that their reactions are normal under the circumstances. Many managers feel uncomfortable when employees openly display emotions and, as a result, respond to basic fears or enthusiasm with rational arguments. Consequently, employees often feel misunderstood or patronized when they finally have the courage to verbalize their concerns.

Managers may think employees overreact or act irrationally in the face of minor problems. Tensions rise instead of being relieved and communication attempts stop. Personnel officers can first provide emotional support to frustrated employees and then assist them in expressing their concerns and fears in constructive ways. Administrators, on the other hand, can be made aware of particular concerns, so that they are not caught totally off guard and are better able to deal with the problems and frustrations expressed.

Major frustrations experienced by personnel officers themselves stem from their inability to please everybody. Many times employees feel relieved about problem situations after they talk to a personnel officer, but when the situation continues to persist, they feel cheated and disappointed. It is a good rule of thumb for personnel officers to always ask all persons if they want any actions taken on their concerns. Usually they will want to think about it but asking will leave the door open for future consultations and makes it clear that the decision to pursue matters is really up to the employee.

Personnel officers can create many frustrations for themselves by not realizing that their role is largely advisory and that they cannot force line administrators to pursue a particular course if they don't want to. Professional and ethical dilemmas develop when personnel officers know about problems, think they know how to resolve them, advise supervisors, but no action is forthcoming. Time and experiences—both good and bad—will prove to be valuable guides in such situations; so will the good counsel of colleagues.

The position of personnel officer can be a most rewarding and fulfilling career choice for many librarians. Besides maturity, understanding of human beings, and knowledge of organizational processes, it requires an ability to balance employees' personnel needs with those of the organization. Personnel officers will want to be a role model by demonstrating the desirability and usefulness of continuing education in preparing themselves for the personnel position. A master's degree in library/information sciences, while not absolutely necessary, is highly desirable. It will foster credibility, and facilitate communication and the understanding of problems germane to libraries.

Additional formal degree programs like the Master's of Business Administration, Master's of Public Administration, and Master's of Higher Education Administration, can provide a foundation of the necessary personnel or organizational skills, as can extensive participation in continuing education programs offered by library professional associations or others. If organizational theory and personnel courses prove not to be of interest, other career options should be explored. Since management theories and concepts are constantly evolving, personnel officers will find it necessary to not only update their own understanding of these developments but provide the opportunities for all employees to learn about them and encourage their implementation.

In libraries in transition, effective personnel officers must be risk takers. While reinforcing and supporting the creative efforts of other administrators, personnel officers themselves need to move the organization forward through their knowledge of organizational and human development, their choices of continuing education programs, and individual counseling efforts.

Since creative endeavors are usually haphazard, open-ended, and unpredictable in terms of outcome, personnel officers in changing organizations need to be able to tolerate a high degree of ambiguity and be unafraid of failure.

At the same time, libraries, even those in transition, are fairly structured organizations and often part of a bigger bureaucracy. This fact imposes obvious limits on any administrator's creativity, and the challenge for all becomes innovative within the constraints set by the parent organization.

As organizational structures evolve and the organizational climate becomes more predictable, the role of a personnel officer will also change. Codification of shared expectations, writing of policies and procedures manuals, and perfecting of training plans and personnel recording keeping systems may become prevalent and the focus of activity.

Outwardly directed concerns with overall organizational issues will most likely be replaced with concerns directly related to the effective functioning of the personnel office. While the day-to-day personnel duties were performed and hopefully improved during the organizational transition, they were not the primary focus of activities. At this point, it may become necessary to hire a new personnel officer, since the one who helped to bring about organizational changes could find the new focus limiting and consider it "paper pushing."

On the other hand this shift of focus may also provide a personnel officer with a welcome opportunity to complete the cycle of change and create for the organization the actual documents proving its evolution. The continuing evaluation and fine-tuning of organizational structures and processes, the provisions for continuing education to meet the needs of the new organization and new employees, and the personal growth of the personnel officer can provide ever-changing perspectives and challenges to the position.

Chapter 9
The Future

Predicting the future is risky and fraught with danger under the best of circumstances; it is especially perilous considering the accelerating rate of change in society today. Making predictions concerning the library profession is no exception. Change will most likely affect librarianship more dramatically than any of us can envision today. The only thing we are certain of is that the changes will continue; the best we can do is to prepare ourselves mentally and physically to be aware, open to new possibilities, and able to cope. The possibilities are all around us: to acquire new skills, improve our mental and physical capacities, be exposed to new experiences, and have old and dear assumptions challenged. Are we willing to consciously risk the status quo and move forward, sometimes by trial and error, or will we wait until we are forced to adapt to changes imposed by others?

REDEFINING ROLES

Librarians are not generally known as proactive. Since it appears that our profession will be entering a period of turbulence, opportunities, and tests, many of us will be faced with exciting or traumatic choices, depending on our outlook. Over the next decade, our role in society can become vitally important if we take charge of filling its informational needs. If we are complacent and satisfied with storing and providing access to information that is usually several years out of date by the time it reaches our libraries, other professions will emerge and assert their claim to fill the gap.

There is no doubt that we will be forced to redefine who we are, what we do, and explain why our profession is needed in the emerging new age. It appears that we have had a lot of practice doing just that over the last 100 years; therefore, analyzing our contribution to and place in society should be easier for us than for many other professionals faced with the same need to analyze their future. After all, we know how to access the data needed and we are intelligent enough to draw the correct conclusions! Are we not?

In this chapter we will try to make some general observations and predictions about issues and concerns we think will emerge or reemerge for consideration or resolution. They are not exhaustive for obvious reasons, but they seem to be looming on the horizon and waiting to be addressed or acknowledged.

WOMEN MANAGERS

A library in transition today will certainly have a number of women managers. Women now in responsible administrative positions have generally had to be flexible, assertive, knowledgeable, team-oriented and self-directed, with large doses of initiative in order to have progressed into management. These are all qualities needed in effective organizations that are ready and willing to address future issues. Women managers will become an increasingly critical force in library administration. By balancing and enriching the traditional management team and challenging old assumptions, they will help change library organizations.

Women managers will represent many of the values, hopes, and ambitions of the majority of library workers, who are female. They will emphasize the development of all human resources as a means to help the organization achieve its goals. Women managers have usually spent years at lower organizational levels. Their actual work experiences will help balance the ideal with the possible. Organizational dynamics will change as women managers rely on concern for others, creativity, and instinct. Through their willingness to verbalize issues, organizational communication will be facilitated. Organizational energy will be saved as issues are addressed sooner.

Managerial opportunities have been denied to women for a considerable time period. Women will place greater emphasis on continuing education and will encourage others to develop their abilities and overcome weaknesses. Women must free themselves from being too closely involved in the day-to-day activities they supervise and see and reflect upon the overall organizational needs.

Women managers will also experience skepticism about their abilities and accusations of inexperience, power plays, and emotional instability. They will have to tolerate threatened male administrators asking: "Little Lady, do you realize the scope of responsibilities this job entails? Do you really think *you* can handle the job?"

UNIONS

The role of unions in libraries, as in other organizations, will change in the future. It appears at the moment that the major growth area for unions is in the public sector. However, that in itself attests to the fact that unions and their membership have to adopt different methods of operating because of the inherent constraints imposed by non-profit environments. The right to strike, for instance, one of the most powerful union sanctions, is often not acknowledged in the public sector.

Non-profit organizations usually do not control the sources of their incomes but are instead dependent on taxation, fees, donations, etc. Nobody in the public sector amasses great fortunes or profits at the expense of labor; rather, management and labor's compensation and benefits are usually regulated by law and are not subject to negotiations.

Because of these and other factors, unions cannot use their traditional confrontational and adversarial approach to labor-management relationships. As libraries evolve into participative environments, both management and labor will cooperatively plan for and determine the future of the organizations. Unions will develop into one of several cooperative forces, providing useful global information and perspectives to foster the ability of libraries and employees to survive and adapt to changing conditions. In librarianship, unions will be used to help educate clientele and the public of the importance of the profession and assist employees and management in adapting positive attitudes toward the required changes. Organizational and professional survival and well-being will become the objective of both management and labor.

FACULTY STATUS

The desirability and practicality of faculty status for academic librarians will continue to be debated for the foreseeable future. We think that a universal solution is neither possible nor desirable. Each library and librarian should consider the options available and make decisions that meet their particular needs.

It may be necessary for those libraries that see faculty status as essential to accomplishing their mission to require staff to complete graduate work at the doctoral level. Some staff not inclined toward scholarship will leave to choose a different organizational or career path. Faculty status appears to create as many problems as it solves, and the library literature attests to valid arguments pro and con. The profession is starting to realize that just as an M.L.S. does not a professional make, so is faculty status no guarantee for respect, input in university affairs, job security, and higher credibility.

True faculty status, like anything else, has its price. Libraries must decide if they have the resources required to implement faculty status. Librarians need to decide if they are willing to meet the necessary criteria to earn the privilege. To be truly equal with the faculty may demand a doctorate in the future, with research and service activities becoming an integral part of our work. If we are not willing to recognize that and continue to insist on the master's degree as the terminal degree in an institution that grants us faculty status, we may remain second-class faculty and have to deal with the resulting frustrations.

Since the profession has experimented with a variety of different appointment statuses in the last 25 years, librarians and libraries faced with making a decision about adopting a certain status should have enough good data on the advantages and disadvantages of each approach. Decisions can be developed jointly between library administrators and staffs, taking into consideration local circumstances.

An appointment status that has received acceptance in many academic communities is that of administrative/professional. This category recognizes the importance of librarians within academia and accords them specific benefits. At the same time librarians with this status within the academic community will need to assert themselves to gain appointment to relevant faculty committees, or they will find that their administrative/professional status excludes them from this vital interaction with faculty. Those librarians with administrative/professional status must also recognize the necessity for professional activities and the resulting visibility so they are not relegated to an administrative clone role.

STAFFING SHORTAGES

Libraries are starting to experience staffing shortages again. Recruitment difficulties for children's librarians and catalogers experienced at this time may become the trend for all professional positions. As already pointed out, the traditional labor pool for librarianship—women—has diminished as female professionals continue to find attractive opportunities in more lucrative fields. In addition, the labor pool generally is shrinking, creating potential recruitment problems for all organizations. Rather than considering this as a major problem, we should view potential staffing shortages as a great opportunity to move the profession forward.

Because of automation, many responsibilities previously held by professionals are now performed by support staff. However, many libraries still continue to have the same number of professionals on staff, as if nothing had changed. Potential staffing shortages will force the profession to continuously evaluate each position, task, and responsibility, and delegate as many routine duties as possible to support staff. The ratio of support staff to professional staff should continue to increase from 2 to 1 to 4 or 5 to 1, minimizing an organization's need to replace each professional with another professional.

Job opportunities for those in the profession and those entering it can be enhanced through these trends, but they will also demand new skills and higher commitments to librarianship as a profession and to lifelong learning. Those viewing librarianship merely as a job, a source of income, a pleasant, undemanding way to make a living will no longer have a place in the profession. Practicing librarians will need to play a greater and more aggressive role in identifying potential professionals in the ranks of support staff and student assistants and actively sell librarianship as an exciting and promising career option.

REORGANIZATIONAL ISSUES

Libraries of all types will be facing many reorganizational needs as the lines blur between departments, as professional and support staff responsibilities change, as staff shortages become more critical, and as automation makes its presence felt. Staff will be working in more than one functional area, developing additional skills and broadening their viewpoint of the organization.

Administrators and managers will be called upon to learn new managerial skills and assume responsibilities outside their areas of emphasis. In some public and academic libraries we already see administrators assuming additional responsibilities in other municipal or county governmental units or in other academic support areas such as the computer area.

Chief executive officers will spend more of their energies and time on external matters to enhance the library's visibility, make known its needs and services, and identify ways the library can better meet the needs of its constituency.

At the same time, the daily library operations must continue. More libraries will be centralizing these internal responsibilities within a deputy director position though the title will vary among different libraries. This consolidation of responsibilities will further blur functional duties and lead to more merging of duties and positions. Elimination of divisional lines and merging of responsibilities under one senior administrator will save hours of negotiation efforts that formerly were necessary when responsibilities and projects crossed divisional lines. Libraries undergoing such a reorganization will find that not only energies and time will be saved but also staff and monies can be redirected to other pursuits that will enable the library to more effectively achieve its mission.

A high level of managerial skills, reflected in specialized training and developed talents, will be required of the manager in a reorganized library. This skills level may not necessarily be reflected in advanced degrees past the master's level but will be found through experience.

MENTAL HEALTH REQUIREMENTS

Managers in libraries in transition find that they have to spend an extraordinary amount of time on personnel issues, often caused by laissez-faire or autocratic managerial practices of the past. Because job expectations for support staff and professionals were often unclear or not adequately communicated, libraries were often unable to establish a good match between positions and applicants.

Good recruitment skills, policies, and procedures are essential to create a new organizational development. But they are not easily developed. "Check-up interviews" conducted with library employees after they have been in their position for three months at our institution usually reveal that most had no idea about the true nature of their positions when they first entered the organization.

Most envisioned the library as a pleasant, stress-free place, where staff read, file cards, check out books, and answer directional questions from the public. Although these people went through a rigorous interviewing process, and received position announcements, job descriptions, and other relevant information before the interview, their perceptions remain clouded by stereotypes. Some have problems letting go of their preconceptions and usually leave or are encouraged to leave during the first year.

Libraries are making progress in communicating their organizational and professional needs during the recruitment process, but many employees are still hired because they are nice, educated, unassertive, and fit into the library environment of the past. The results are personnel problems caused by employees who cannot cope with new requirements for well-developed managerial and intellectual skills and constantly changing expectations.

Finding ways to help new and long-term employees deal with the frustrations and stresses created by the new demands requires much organizational energy. Managers must become adept at balancing organizational and personal needs of employees and providing problem employees with alternatives and choices. Librarians are not trained as counselors but can provide information sources that can assist with problems. It will be much more helpful to individuals with problems to be referred to personnel specialists, employee assistance programs, and counseling centers than to be ignored.

The use of committees in the recruitment of all personnel can minimize the hiring of problem employees. Including some long-term employees who have work performance problems in the committees may not sound like a good idea, but in our experience, problem employees often are drawn to each other, filling each other's emotional needs. If a committee expresses some uneasiness about a particular candidate, a manager can check if the person received a strong recommendation to be hired from a problem employee and advise the committee to try to determine the underlying reasons for their own hesitation in recommending hiring. A second interview, incorporating careful reference checks and the addition of employees in the hiring process, may provide additional insights and prevent the committee from saddling the organization with yet another problem.

AUTOMATION AND INFORMATION BROKERAGE

Libraries have embraced automation, welcoming it as a panacea for many problems. While automation is an integral part of libraries and will increasingly become a key component for library planning and reorganization, automation should be viewed realistically as a tool the library can use to achieve its mission. Librarians should use automation to enhance libraries' role as an information access point.

New technology incorporating automation allows libraries to store information in less space-consuming means, thus preserving knowledge for future generations without relying on the concept of warehousing physical materials and constantly increasing facilities storage. At the same time, the new storage media and online access to the library's database of holdings and to commercial subject-oriented databases broaden the ability to access information and allow dispersal of information access outside the library. Libraries will assume the role of information broker.

The special training librarians receive, coupled with the use of automation, will lead to new types of positions within and without libraries that allow librarians to apply their skills to develop new databases and create interactive software to accomplish some library activities, such as library instruction, use of certain library tools, and training purposes.

The enlargement of librarians' and libraries' use of—and reliance upon—automation will require that computer literacy become part of our training for library staff. Just as most newspapers of any size have virtually banished typewriters from their premises, libraries and their staff will find themselves incorporating technology into their work place at an accelerating pace.

CONCLUSION

While we can hypothesize about the future of libraries, we cannot fully comprehend what the new challenges and opportunities will be. For most of us, the rest of our careers will be spent in libraries undergoing change, libraries in transition. Whether we enter administrative/managerial positions or pursue operational-level positions, we will all be involved in the process. Knowledge of what we can anticipate and how we will grow from the challenges and opportunities will make the path a positive experience.

Selected Bibliography

Argyris, Chris. *Integrating the Individual and the Organization.* New York: John Wiley & Sons, 1964.

Arthur, Michael B., et al. *Working with Careers.* New York: Center for Research in Career Development, Graduate School of Business, Columbia University, 1984.

Bailey, Martha J. *The Special Librarian as a Supervisor or Middle Manager.* Washington, DC: Special Libraries Association, 1986.

Balachandran, Sarojini. "Recruitment Advertising and Academic Library Directorships," *Journal of Library Administration* 2 (Spring 1981): 25–33.

Belker, Loren B. *The First-Time Manager: A Practical Guide to the Management of People.* New York: AMACOM, 1986.

Bellman, Geoffrey M. *The Quest for Staff Leadership.* Glenview, IL: Scott, Foresman, 1986.

Below, Patrick J.; Morrisey, George L.; and Acomb, Betty L. *The Executive Guide to Strategic Planning.* San Francisco: Jossey-Bass Publishers, 1987.

Berg, Per-Olof. "Symbolic Management of Human Resources," *Human Resource Management* 25 (Winter 1986): 557–79.

Burgelman, Robert A., and Sayles, Leonard R. *Inside Corporate Innovation: Strategy, Structure, and Managerial Skills.* New York: The Free Press, 1986.

Burke, W. Warner. *Organization Development: A Normative View.* Reading, MA: Addison-Wesley Publishing Company, 1987.

Cargill, Jennifer. "Technical Services Automation: The Human Factor." Paper presented at the Ohio Valley Group of Technical Services Librarians Conference, Berea, KY, May 1986.

Cherrington, David S. *Work Ethics: Working Values and Values that Work.* New York: AMACOM, 1980.

Cohen, Herb. *You Can Negotiate Anything.* New York: Bantam Books, 1980.

Cohen, Michael D., and March, James G. *Leadership and Ambiguity: The American College President.* 2d ed. Boston: Harvard Business School Press, 1986.

Conroy, Barbara. "The Human Element: Staff Development in the Electronic Library." *Drexel Library Quarterly* 17 (Fall 1981): 91–106.

Darling, John R., and Cluff, E. Dale. "Managing Interpersonal Conflict in a University Library." *Library Administration and Management* 1 (January 1987): 16–22.

————. "Social Styles and the Art of Managing Up." *The Journal of Academic Librarianship* 12 (January 1987): 350–55.

Fisher, K. Kim. "Management Roles in the Implementation of Participative Management Systems." *Human Resource Management* 25 (Fall 1986): 459–79.

Foster, Richard N. *Innovation: the Attacker's Advantage.* New York: Summit Books, 1986.

Gehrman, Douglas B. "The Deregulated Employee." *Personnel Administrator* 31 (January 1986): 35–40.

Gibson, Jane Whitney, and Hodgetts, Richard M. *Organizational Communication: A Managerial Perspective.* Orlando, FL: Academic Press, 1986.

Golembiewski, Robert. "Mid-Life Transition and Mid-Career Crisis: A Special Case for Individual Development." *Public Administration Review* 38 (March/April 1978): 215–22.

Gould, J., and Kolb, William A., eds. *A Dictionary of the Social Sciences.* New York: The Free Press, 1964.

Hersey, Paul, and Blanchard, Kenneth H. *Management of Organizational Behavior: Utilizing Human Resources.* 3d ed. Englewood Cliffs, NJ: Prentice-Hall, 1977.

Hornstein, Harvey A. *Managerial Courage.* New York: John Wiley & Sons, 1986.

Hyatt, James A., and Santiago, Aurora A. *University Libraries in Transition.* Washington, DC: National Association of College and University Business Officers, 1987.

Kanter, Rosabeth Moss. *The Change Masters: Innovation and Entrepreneurship in the American Corporation.* New York: Simon & Schuster, 1983.

————. "The New Workforce Meets the Changing Workplace: Strains, Dilemmas, and Contradictions in Attempts to Implement Participative and Entrepreneurial Management." *Human Resource Management* 25 (Winter 1986): 515–37.

Katzell, Raymond, and Yankelovich, Daniel. *Work, Productivity, and Job Satisfaction: An Evaluation of Policy-Related Research.* New York: The Psychological Corporation, 1975.

Kets de Vries, Manfred, et al. "Using the Life Cycle to Anticipate Satisfaction at Work." *Journal of Forecasting* 3 (2) (1984): 161–72.

Lakein, Alan. *How to Get Control of Your Time and Your Life.* New York: New American Library, 1973.

Lewis, David W. "An Organizational Paradigm for Effective Academic Libraries." *College and Research Libraries* 47 (July 1986): 337–53.

Likert, Rensis. *The Human Organization: Its Management and Value.* New York: McGraw-Hill, 1967.

————. *New Patterns of Management.* New York: McGraw-Hill, 1961.

Losoncy, Lewis. *The Motivating Leader.* Englewood Cliffs, NJ: Prentice-Hall, 1985.

Lowry, Charles B. "Technology in Libraries: Six Rules for Management." *Library Hi Tech* 3 (1985): 27–29.

McGregor, Douglas. *The Human Side of Enterprise.* New York: McGraw-Hill, 1960.

————. *The Professional Manager.* New York: McGraw-Hill, 1967.

Maccoby, Michael. *The Leader.* New York: Simon & Schuster, 1981.

————. "Leadership Needs of the 1980s." *Current Issues in Higher Education* 1 (1979): 17–23.

Mackenzie, R. Alec. *The Time Trap: How to Get More Done in Less Time.* New York: McGraw-Hill, 1972.

Maslow, A. H. *Motivation and Personality.* New York: Harper & Brothers, 1954.

Matejko, Alexander. *The Self-Defeating Organization.* New York: Praeger, 1986.

Miles, Raymond E. *Theories of Management: Implications for Organizational Behavior and Development.* New York: McGraw-Hill, 1975.

Millett, John D. *Management, Governance and Leadership.* New York: AMACOM, 1980.

Monden, Yasuhiro, et al. *Innovations in Management: The Japanese Corporation.* Norcross, GA: Industrial Engineering and Management Press, 1985.

Morf, Martin. *Optimizing Work Performance: A Look Beyond the Bottom Line.* New York: Quorum Books, 1986.

Naisbitt, John. *Megatrends: Ten New Directions Transforming Our Lives.* New York: Warner, 1984.

Olsgaard, John N. "Automation as a Socio-Organizational Agent of Change: An Evaluative Literature Review." *Information Technology and Libraries* 4 (March 1985): 19–28.

Ouchi, William G. *Theory Z: How American Business Can Meet the Challenge of Japanese Management.* Reading, MA: Addison-Wesley, 1981.

Pascarella, Perry. *The New Achievers: Creating a Modern Work Ethic.* New York: Free Press, 1984.

Peters, Tom, and Austin, Nancy. *A Passion for Excellence: The Leadership Difference.* New York: Warner Books, Inc., 1985.

Peters, Tom, and Waterman, Robert H. J. *In Search of Excellence.* New York: Harper & Row, 1982.

Plumez, Jacqueline H. *Divorcing a Corporation: How to Know When-and-If a Job Change Is Right for You.* New York: Villard Books, 1986.

Portnoy, Robert A. *Leadership: What Every Leader Should Know about People.* Englewood Cliffs, NJ: Prentice-Hall, 1986.

Prytherch, Ray. *Handbook of Library Training Practice.* Aldershot, England: Gower Publishing Company Limited, 1986.

Quick, Thomas L. *Inspiring People at Work: How to Make Participative Management Work for You.* New York: Executive Enterprises Publications, 1986.

———. *Managing People at Work Desk Guide.* New York: Executive Enterprises Publications, 1983.

Rasberry, Robert W., and Lemoine, Laura Fletcher. *Effective Managerial Communication.* Boston: Kent Publishing, 1986.

Riggs, Donald E. *Library Leadership: Visualizing the Future.* Phoenix, AZ: Oryx Press, 1982.

———. *Strategic Planning for Library Managers.* Phoenix, AZ: Oryx Press, 1984.

———. *Time Management Study in Academic Libraries.* Washington, DC: Council on Library Resources, 1986.

Roberson, Cliff. *Preventing Employee Misconduct: A Self-Defense Manual for Businesses.* Lexington, MA: Lexington Books, 1986.

Sayles, Leonard R. *Leadership: What Effective Managers Really Do...and How They Do It.* New York: McGraw-Hill, 1979.

Schneier, Craig Eric; Beatty, Richard W.; and McEnvoy, Glenn M. *Personnel/Human Resources Management Today: Readings and Commentary.* 2d ed. Reading, MA: Addison-Wesley, 1986.

Schott, Richard L. "The Psychological Developments of Adults: Implications for Public Administration." *Public Administration Review* 46 (November/December 1986): 657-67.

Schuler, Randall S. "Fostering and Facilitating Entrepreneurship in Organizations: Implications for Organization Structure and Human Resource Management Practices." *Human Resource Management* 25 (Winter 1986): 607-29.

Shapero, Albert. *Managing Professional People.* New York: Free Press, 1985.

Simon, Herbert A. *Administrative Behavior.* 3d ed. New York: Free Press, 1976.

Stewart, Douglas. *The Power of People Skills: A Manager's Guide to Assessing and Developing Your Organization's Greatest Resource.* New York: John Wiley & Sons, 1986.

Tinsley, Adrian; Secor, Cynthia; and Kaplan, Sheila. *Women in Higher Education Administration*. San Francisco, CA: Jossey-Bass, 1984.

Toffler, Alvin. *The Third Wave*. New York: Bantam Books, 1980.

Webb, Gisela, and Cargill, Jennifer. "Employee Assistance Programs: A Positive Approach to the Problem Employee." *LAMA Newsletter* 12 (June 1986): 65–68.

White, Herbert S. *Education for Professional Librarians*. White Plains, NY: Knowledge Industry, 1986.

———. *Library Personnel Management*. White Plains, NY: Knowledge Industry, 1985.

Williams, Delmus E. and Racine, Drew. "Planning for Evaluation: The Concept of Pre-evaluation." *LAMA Newsletter* 11 (September 1985): 73–75.

Wren, Daniel A. *The Evolution of Management Thought*. 2d ed. New York: John Wiley & Sons, 1979.

Wynn, Richard and Guditus, Charles W. *Team Management: Leadership by Consensus*. Columbus, OH: Charles E. Merrill, 1984.

Yankelovich, Daniel. *New Rules, Searching for Self-Fulfillment in a World Turned Upside Down*. New York: Random House, 1981.

Yukl, Gary A. *Leadership in Organizations*. Englewood Cliffs, NJ: Prentice-Hall, 1981.

Zuboff, Shoshana. "New Worlds of Computer-Mediated Work," *Harvard Business Review* 60 (September-October 1982): 142–52.

AUDIO-VISUAL MATERIALS

The ABC's of Decision Making [Videorecording] Des Moines, IA: Creative Media, 1974, 1 cassette, 30 min., ¾ in., color.

Communicating Successfully [Videorecording] New York: Time-Life Video, 1973, 1 cassette, 25 min., ¾ in., color.

Communication: The Nonverbal Agenda [Videorecording] Del Mar, CA: CRM McGraw-Hill Films, 1974, 1 cassette, 31 min., ¾ in., color.

Communication Is You the Discussion Leader [Videorecording] Lincoln, NE: Great Plains National, 1978, 1 cassette, 30 min., ¾ in., color.

Communication Skills for Managers [Videorecording] New York: Time-Life Video, 1980, 6 cassettes, 30 min. each, ¾ in., color.

Creative Problem Solving: How to Get Better Ideas [Videorecording] Del Mar, CA: CRM McGraw-Hill Films, 1979, 1 cassette, 28 min., ¾ in., color.

Everyone's a Negotiator [Videorecording] Wilmette, IL: Films Incorporated, 1980, 1 cassette, 71 min., ¾ in., color.

Finding Time [Videorecording] Del Mar, CA: CRM McGraw-Hill Film, 1980, 1 cassette, 28 min., ¾ in., color.

Living with Stress [Videorecording] Columbus, OH: Xerox Corporation, 1977, 1 cassette, 22 min., ¾ in., color.

Managing Stress [Videorecording] Del Mar, CA: CRM McGraw-Hill Films, 1978, 1 cassette, 35 min., ¾ in., color.

MBO: Management by Objectives and Performance Appraisal [Videorecording] New York: Time-Life Multimedia, 1975, 1 cassette, 45 min., ¾ in., color.

A New Look at Motivation [Videorecording] Del Mar, CA: CRM McGraw-Hill Films, 1980, 1 cassette, 32 min., ¾ in., color.

The Nuts and Bolts of Performance Appraisal [Videorecording] Del Mar, CA: CRM McGraw-Hill Films, 1973, 1 cassette, 32 min., ¾ in., color.

The One Minute Manager [Videorecording] Wilmette, IL: Films Incorporated, 1983, 1 cassette, 50 min., ¾ in., color.

Perception [Videorecording] Del Mar, CA: CRM McGraw-Hill Films, 1979, 1 cassette, 27 min., ¾ in., color.

Performance Appraisal: The Human Dynamics [Videorecording] Del Mar, CA: CRM McGraw-Hill Films, 1978, 1 cassette, 25 min., ¾ in., color.

Performance Appraisal for Managers [Videorecording] New York: Time-Life Video, 1981, 7 cassettes, 30 min. each, ¾ in., color.

Persuasive Negotiating [Videorecording] Wilmette, IL: Films Incorporated, 1981, 1 cassette, 60 min., ¾ in., color.

The Power of Listening [Videorecording] Del Mar, CA: CRM McGraw-Hill Films, 1978, 1 cassette, 26 min., ¾ in., color.

Problem Solving Strategies: The Synectics Approach [Videorecording] Del Mar, CA: CRM McGraw-Hill Films, 1980, 1 cassette, 27 min., ¾ in., color.

Productivity and the Self-fulfilling Prophecy: The Pygmalion Effect [Videorecording] Del Mar, CA: CRM McGraw-Hill Films, 1975, 1 cassette, 29 min., ¾ in., color.

Stress Management: A Positive Strategy [Videorecording] New York: Time-Life Video, 1982, 5 cassettes, 30 min. each, ¾ in., color.

Time Management for Managers [Videorecording] New York: Time-Life Video, 1980, 6 cassettes, 45 min. each, ¾ in., color.

The Time of Your Life [Videorecording] Hollywood, CA: Cally Curtis Co., 1974, 1 cassette, 26 min., ¾ in., color.

Transactional Analysis [Videorecording] Del Mar, CA: CRM McGraw-Hill Films, 1974, 1 cassette, 33 min., ¾ in., color.

Understanding Behavior in Organizations: How I Feel Is What I Do [Videorecording] New York: Document Associates, 1977, 1 cassette, 26 min., ¾ in., color.

What You Are Is.... [Videorecording] Wilmette, IL: Films Incorporated, 1982, 3 cassettes, 90 min., ¾ in., color.

Women in Management: Threat or Opportunity? [Videorecording] Del Mar, CA: CRM McGraw-Hill Films, 1975, 1 cassette, 30 min., ¾ in., color.

Appendix:
Staff Management Tools

Example of a Training Program

This program can be modified for different levels of staffing and as appropriate for the complexity of the position's assignments.

CATALOG LIBRARIAN TRAINING PROGRAM

In order to provide a realistic retraining program, the following job tasks are presented in the sequence listed, starting with the simplest task and progressing to the tasks set forth for any nonadministrative catalog librarian. While one experienced cataloger has been assigned as the advisor/revisor/resource person, other personnel should be consulted as needed.

Task 1

Edited Records:

The first job task is assigning call numbers, assigning and/or verifying subject headings, and checking all other fields of the edited records, or printouts of incomplete records located in the database.

Expectations:

Most of these records are cataloged with the AACR2 rules but are not complete. Review of the records with the books in hand will provide initial introduction to the variations in the AACR2 rules as well as the tagging elements of the OCLC cataloging subsystem. This task will also allow the trainee to become reacquainted with the LC classification tables, the LC subject headings, cataloging tools, and the OCLC terminal. The trainee would be expected to start with the easier records as selected by his or her advisor/revisor and progress to the more difficult. During this time the trainee will be expected to learn searching techniques in OCLC and NUC and also learn the name authority subsystem for the verification of corporate, personal, series, and place name verification for the AACR2 form.

Time Frame:

With the trainee spending 100 percent of his or her time in this activity, the acceptable accuracy rate will progress to 90–95 percent by the end of the time limit set for this task. Six weeks should be sufficient for this first phase of training before moving on to the next task. However, edited records will not cease to be part of the work assignment.

Task 2

Retrospective Conversion:

The second task will be the upgrading of the cataloging of monographs from the Retro Project for original inputting into the OCLC database.

Expectations:

Since the item has already been cataloged, the task will provide an easier transition from the edited records to filling out a tag sheet for original input. The tag sheets must be in compliance with AACR2 rules, LC variations and practices included, and the OCLC rules as set forth in the book's format. Also, all subject and name authority work must be completed.

Time Frame:

The trainee will be expected to be 90 percent accurate at the end of one month for this task before moving on to the next level. Retrospective conversion, as with edited records, will become a facet of the ongoing work assignment.

Task 3

Original Cataloging:

The third task will be original cataloging. All of the previously required knowledge will be used in the accomplishment of this task.

Expectations:

In the first task, the learning of the LC classification schedules will be applied. In all steps the assigning of LC subject headings is a possibility. The tag sheet for original cataloging will be the same as for the original input of Retro items. The trainee will be expected to fill out tag sheets for new items (not found in OCLC or LC) correctly. Again they must be in accordance with rules and procedures as previously stated. The trainee will be expected to catalog those items of subject expertise and progress to other areas.

Time Frame:

The trainee will be expected to hit a 95 percent proficiency rate at the end of one month before progressing to the next level.

Task 4

Revision:

All of the above tasks, if accomplished within the three-and-a-half month time period, will provide the trainee with all necessary background to advance to the fourth task of revision of the original cataloging and/or original input of the Retro Project of an assigned cataloger.

Expectations:

The trainee will be expected to proof the tag sheets of an assigned cataloger for cataloging, tagging, and name authority work, making sure all is in compliance with rules as set forth in Task 2. Any major changes deemed necessary by the revisor must be discussed with the cataloger for mutual consent.

Time Frame:

No time is specified; no new tasks are learned in this task.

Task 5

Problem Solving:

The problem-solving and special-assigned projects are the last part of any catalog librarian's job. These are the special functions that crop up and are shared by the department as a whole. A trainee able to accomplish the first four steps should have no problem.

Basis for Time Frames and Expectations:

New library school students are expected to learn the AACR2 rules and original cataloging procedures in a class meeting three hours a week for one semester. Trainees working three-and-a-half months for 8-hour days should, therefore, be accomplished catalogers, able to be productive and accurate members of the Catalog Department.

As each task is learned, it will become a part of the ongoing work assignment.

Affirmative Action Library Assistant Training Plan

INTRODUCTION

This training program is designed to provide on-the-job training to employees in Library Assistant I and II positions to increase specific skills necessary for promotion into upward classification when vacancies occur within the library. It will also benefit the library by upgrading employee skills to enhance productivity and efficiency. Typically employees in lower position classifications have narrowly defined job responsibilities and lack opportunities to develop other skills. Their knowledge of other library departments and functions is limited because of their own narrow job focus.

SELECTION

The candidates will be selected in accordance with affirmative action guidelines, which are designed to diversify the work force among all job categories and classes. A total of up to four library assistants will be chosen each time by the Assistant Director of Libraries for Personnel Service in conjunction with the individual unit heads releasing the participants for training. Selection will be based on the following criteria:

1. Motivation to participate, as demonstrated by filling out an application form on which reasons for participation are outlined;
2. Unsuccessful attempts at applying for higher library positions;
3. Length of employment within their current classifications; and
4. Affirmative action considerations.

LENGTH AND NATURE OF PROGRAM

Training programs will last a total of six months, with employees being trained in *one* public service department and *one* technical service department for three months each. Employees chosen will work for three hours each day for 15 hours per week in the assigned department. The Assistant Director for Personnel Services will choose the training department based on the employee's preference and the willingness of the chosen departments to participate.

Upon completion of the training program each trainee will have at least two of the following skills:

1. Order or precataloging of books or periodicals using the OCLC bibliographic utility;

2. Use of OCLC or CLSI bibliographic records and other tools to assist library patrons in public service areas;

3. Input records in either the OCLC bibliographic network or CLSI;

4. Perform other responsibilities as assigned by his or her trainers.

TRAINERS

The trainers will be selected by the department head in each department based on their ability and willingness to participate in the program. The trainers will prepare training plans for each trainee and evaluate the progress of participants weekly. If problems develop, trainers and trainees will consult with the Assistant Director for Personnel Services, who will involve others as needed.

EVALUATIONS

After the completion of each three-month segment of the training program both trainers and trainees will be asked to evaluate the success of the program and suggest modifications, as needed. Evaluations will try to establish:

1. Whether the participants perceive that carrying out the training activities significantly enhanced their skills and developed potential for upward mobility;

2. Whether supervisors and trainers involved in the training activity perceived that utilizing newly acquired skills significantly enhanced the participant's ability and potential for upward mobility; and

3. Whether the participant's department head perceived that the new skills significantly enhanced the trainee's current job performance and potential for upward mobility.

OTHER

After the training program has been completed, the candidates will resume their normal working schedule with no guarantee of placement into a higher classification position.

Participating departments may ask for an increase in student assistant budget allocations to compensate for the time trainers and trainees are unavailable for their usual work. The increase requested should not exceed 15 hours per department.

Employees already in the library will facilitate organizational communication and understanding of mutual concerns and constraints. This program will broaden employee perspectives about the organizational mission and goals and build an appreciation for the contribution of colleagues and coworkers.

Example of a Staff Recognition Program

The Library has a competent and dedicated staff. The Staff Recognition Program is designed to provide recognition to employees whose demonstrated job performance can be described as "excellent and above and beyond the call of duty," and who best exemplify the outstanding characteristics and the dedication of all library staff.

EMPLOYEE OF THE YEAR AWARD

a. Eligibility: Candidates must be current, benefits-eligible employees of the library. Members of the Administrative Council are ineligible. The recipient will be chosen from among the four persons receiving the "Most Valued Employee" award in their respective area (see page 181).

b. Selection Criteria: Outstanding job performance, competence, exceptional commitment to the job; self motivation, creativity and innovation, cooperation with fellow employees, positive attitude, and library service.

c. Selection Procedures: The recipient will be chosen by a selection committee composed of one representative from each area headed by a member of the Administrative Council, excepting the Director's Office and Personnel. These areas, as currently structured, include Administrative Services, Reference and Instruction, Special Collection/Rare Books and Technical Processing. Employees working in the excepted areas will be considered a part of Administrative Services.

The committee members will be elected by the staff from each area by July 30th of each year. Representatives may be reelected. The Committee will select its own chairperson. The recipient's name will be forwarded to the Director of Libraries by August 30th of each year.

d. Presentation: The Director of Libraries will present the award to the employee at a ceremony to be held in early September of each year.

e. The award consists of the recipient's name being placed on a permanent plaque, which will be exhibited in a prominent place, an individual plaque, a certificate of appreciation, a letter from the Director of Libraries, and $150.00.

MOST VALUED EMPLOYEE IN [insert division] AWARD

a. Eligibility: Candidates must be current, benefits-eligible employees of a functional area headed by a member of the Administrative Council, excepting the Director's Office and Personnel. Functional areas as currently structured include Administrative Services, Reference and Instruction, Special Collection/Rare Books and Technical Processing. The employees working in the excepted areas will be considered a part of Administrative Services for this purpose. Members of the Administrative Council are ineligible.

b. Selection Criteria: Outstanding job performance, competence, exceptional commitment to the job, self motivation, creativity and innovation, cooperation with fellow employees, positive attitude, and university/library service.

c. Selection Procedures: Nominations for awards will be solicited from the staff in each area as defined on page 182–83. The person receiving the most nominations will be the recipient of the award. Nomination forms are available in the library's personnel office and should be returned to that office by May 20th of each year. The recipients' names will be forwarded to the Committee for the Employee of the Year Award by July 30th of each year.

d. Presentation: The respective Associate/Assistant Directors will present the awards at a ceremony to be held in early September of each year.

e. The award for each recipient will consist of a book, a certificate of appreciation, and a letter from the respective Administrative Council Member.

ATTENDANCE RECOGNITION

a. Eligibility: Candidates must be current, benefits-eligible employees of the library and have been employed for at least one full year. Members of the Administrative Council are ineligible.
b. Selection Criteria: Amount of sick leave used during the previous fiscal year. All persons who used zero sick leave and/or the three persons who used the least amount will receive the awards.
c. Selection Procedures: Library personnel will check the sick leave records and confirm the records with respective Administrative Council members and the Central Personnel Records department. Names of candidates will be sent to the Director of Libraries by August 30th of each year.
d. Presentation: The Director of Libraries will present the awards at a ceremony to be held in early September of each year.
e. The award will consist of a certificate of appreciation and a letter from the Director of Libraries.

OUTSTANDING STUDENT ASSISTANT AWARD

a. Eligibility: Candidates must have worked as a student assistant, either work-study or non-work-study, for at least one full semester.
b. Selection Criteria: Job performance, competence, dependability, cooperation with fellow employees.
c. Selection Procedure: The recipient will be determined by a selection committee composed of one representative from each area headed by a member of the Administrative Council, excepting the Personnel and the Director's Office. The Committee will consist of student assistant supervisors recommended by their respective Associate/Assistant Directors. It will convene by August 1st of each year, choose its own chairperson, and accept nominations from other student assistant supervisors until August 15th of each year. Nomination forms will be available in the library's personnel office and should be sent to the Outstanding Student Assistant Awards Committee. The Committee will forward its nominees to the Director of Libraries by August 30th of each year.
d. Presentation: The student assistant supervisor of the nominee will present the award at a ceremony in early September of each year.
e. The award will consist of a set of pens, a certificate of appreciation, and a letter from the student's supervisor.

YEARS OF SERVICE RECOGNITION

a. Eligibility: Candidates must be current, benefits-eligible employees of the library.
b. Selection Criteria: Years of service in five-year increments.
c. Selection Procedures: Library personnel will check the longevity records, confirm the records with respective Administrative Council members and the Central Personnel Records department. Names of people with 5, 10, 15, 20, 25 and more than 30 years of service will be sent to the Director of Libraries by August 30th of each year.
d. Presentation:The Director of Libraries will present pins, certificates of appreciation, and letters from the Director of Libraries.

EMPLOYEE OF THE YEAR AWARD
Selection Form

Name _____ Classification _____

Dept. _____

Beginning Employment Date _____

Give a brief description of candidate's duties and activities.

_____

_____

_____

_____

Candidates for "Employee of the Year Award" will be evaluated on the following criteria. Please address each of the criteria with a brief written description in the space provided.

1. Job Performance:

_____

_____

_____

2. Competence:

_____

_____

_____

3. Commitment to the Job:

_____

_____

_____

4. Self-Motivation:

_____

_____

_____

5. Creativity and Innovation:

_____

_____

_____

6. Cooperation with Fellow Employees:

_____

_____

_____

7. Positive Attitude:

_____

_____

_____

8. Library Service:

_____

_____

_____

Why this person is qualified to be selected as "Employee of the Year."_____

_____

MOST VALUED EMPLOYEE IN [insert division] AWARD
Nomination Form

Name _____ Classification _____

Dept. _____

Beginning Employment Date _____

Candidates for "Most Valued Employee in [insert division] Award" will be evaluated on the following criteria. Please address each of the criteria with a brief written description in the space provided.

1. Job Performance:

_____

_____

_____

2. Competence:

_____

_____

_____

3. Commitment to the Job:

_____

_____

_____

4. Self-Motivation:

_____

_____

_____

5. Creativity and Innovation:

_____

_____

_____

6. Cooperation with Fellow Employees:

_____

_____

_____

7. Positive Attitude:

_____

_____

_____

8. Library Service:

_____

_____

_____

Please explain why you feel this person is qualified to be nominated for the "Most Valued Employee in [insert division] Award."

_____

_____

Please sign your name so we may contact you for further information.

| NAME | DEPT. | DATE |

Examples of Appraisal Materials for Professional Librarians

APPRAISAL CALENDAR

Date	Action
September 1–30	Conference between librarian and his or her supervisor to discuss relevant goals for the academic year and to update the librarian's job description.
January 1–31	Informal discussion of progress toward goals between librarian and his or her supervisor.
March 1–31	Completion of "Statement of Primary Activities." This is a concise report of the librarian's major activities. Each librarian gives this report to his or her supervisor by the first of April.
April 1–30	Evaluations of: (1) librarians by supervisors (2) supervisors by librarians (3) supervisors by supervisors.
May 1–31	Appraisal interviews between librarians being evaluated and evaluators.

STATEMENT OF PRIMARY ACTIVITIES (to be done in March)

The Statement of Primary Activities is a brief, concise report of the librarian's major activities. Each librarian completes this report during March, giving the report to his or her supervisor by the first of April.

A. Give a brief, concise statement of your primary activities, as reflected in your current job description.

B. Give a brief, concise statement of service on departmental, library, or university committees, attendance at conferences/workshops, memberships in and/or committee assignments for professional associations, and any publications/presentations or grants.

C. Describe any progress toward previously stated goals and expectations (which may or may not be discussed in A or B); for example, progress on continuing or ongoing projects.

LIBRARIAN'S PROGRESS AND PLANNING REPORT

Purpose:

The primary purpose of this report is to promote professional growth and development, to enhance general interaction between librarians and their supervisors, to evaluate present work habits, to establish guidelines for continuing performance, and to encourage departmental improvements. This report should be used in conjunction with a *current job description.*

Explanation of Performance Level Scale:

Excellent performance: consistently performs at a level exceptionally above that required of the position.

Exceeds position requirements: usually performs at a level significantly above that required of the position.

Meets position requirements: consistently performs at a level expected of the position as delineated in the job description.

Improvement needed: performance is occasionally less than that required of the position.

Unsatisfactory performance: assessed only if the individual fails to achieve an appropriate degree of improvement in response to an evaluation of "improvement needed" during the previous rating period.

Not applicable: criterion is not related to the individual's role (or job description) and may be indicated without prejudice to the individual's performance.

Librarian's Progress and Planning Report
Form A - A Supervisor Evaluates a Librarian

NAME: _____

UNIT: _____

TITLE: _____

DATES OF COVERAGE: 19 –19

1. QUANTITY OF WORK (quantity of acceptable work completed within reasonable time limitations).

LEVEL OF PERFORMANCE_____

_____

COMMENTS: _____

_____

_____

_____

2. QUALITY OF WORK (accuracy; creativity; reliability; thoroughness; knowledge of principles relating to job performance; ability to interpret and integrate; ability to set priorities).

LEVEL OF PERFORMANCE _____

_____

COMMENTS: _____

_____

_____

_____

3. ATTITUDE (cooperation with others to further the objectives of the unit; willingness to fill in for colleagues when necessary; receptivity to suggestions; adaptability).

LEVEL OF PERFORMANCE _____

_____

COMMENTS: _____

_____

_____

_____

4. INITIATIVE (extra efforts to attain goals; seeks better ways to achieve results; creative thinking; resourceful).

LEVEL OF PERFORMANCE _____

_____

COMMENTS: _____

_____

_____

_____

5. COMMUNICATION AND PERSONAL RELATIONS (ability to work effectively with colleagues and patrons; ability to give clear and concise instructions).

LEVEL OF PERFORMANCE _____

_____

COMMENTS: _____

_____

_____

_____

6. DEPENDABILITY (ability and willingness to follow instructions, meet deadlines, and fulfill responsibilities without direct supervision; punctuality with respect to daily work schedules).

LEVEL OF PERFORMANCE _____

_____

COMMENTS: _____

_____

_____

_____

7. OVERALL PERFORMANCE.

LEVEL OF PERFORMANCE _____

_____

COMMENTS: _____

_____

_____

_____

8. OTHER PERTINENT INFORMATION.

_____

_____

Signature of Librarian Being Evaluated _____

Date _____

Signature of Evaluator _____

Date _____

Reviewed by: _____

Higher-Level Supervisor (initial & date) _____

Director of Libraries (initial & date) _____

(Return to Assistant Director of Libraries for Personnel Services)

Librarian's Progress and Planning Report
Form B - A Librarian evaluates his or her supervisor or One
Supervisor evaluates another Supervisor

NAME: _____

UNIT: _____

TITLE: _____

DATES OF COVERAGE: 19 - 19

1. LEADERSHIP (ability to create an atmosphere that encourages employees to achieve goals; setting an appropriate example for employees; ability to motivate others).

LEVEL OF PERFORMANCE _____

_____

COMMENTS: _____

_____

_____

_____

2. PLANNING AND ORGANIZING (setting priorities and performing important tasks first; ability to identify goals and organize work patterns to achieve these goals; delegates authority and responsibility when appropriate).

LEVEL OF PERFORMANCE _____

_____

COMMENTS: _____

_____

_____

3. DECISION MAKING (ability to identify problems, solicit suggestions, and formulate strategies for problem solving; consistency of judgment; anticipates potential problems).

LEVEL OF PERFORMANCE _____

_____

COMMENTS: _____

_____

_____

_____

4. COMMUNICATIVE SKILLS (encourages two-way communication; ability to instruct clearly; open to suggestions; approachable; ability to work with other units).

LEVEL OF PERFORMANCE _____

_____

COMMENTS: _____

_____

5. SUPERVISORY SKILLS (fairness and impartiality toward staff members; willingness to recognize and resolve grievances; recognition of meritorious achievement, giving proper credit for the ideas and work of individuals/groups; ability to provide appropriate insight and assistance to facilitate problem solving for employees; encourages the professional advancement of employees).

LEVEL OF PERFORMANCE _____

_____

COMMENTS: _____

_____

6. OVERALL PERFORMANCE _____

LEVEL OF PERFORMANCE _____

_____

COMMENTS: _____

_____

7. OTHER PERTINENT INFORMATION

_____

_____

Signature of Librarian Being Evaluated

Date _____

_____

Signature of Evaluator

Date _____

Reviewed by: _____

Higher-Level Supervisor (initial & date) _____

Director of Libraries (initial & date) _____

(Return to Assistant Director of Libraries for Personnel Services)

ADMINISTRATOR EVALUATION FORM

NAME OF ADMINISTRATOR BEING EVALUATED: _____

DATE: _____

NAME OF EVALUATOR: _____

DIRECTIONS: Evaluate each item using the following performance levels: 1 - Excellent performance; 2 - Exceeds position requirements; 3 - Meets position requirements; 4 - Improvement needed; 5 - Unsatisfactory performance; C - Cannot judge; N/A - Not applicable. Please attach at least one example of a deficiency for each 4 and 5 rating.

ADMINISTRATIVE SKILLS

Factors evaluated	Rating
1. Displays effective planning ability.	_____
2. Listens to new ideas.	_____
3. Establishes appropriate goals and objectives.	_____
4. Defines priorities.	_____
5. Clearly defines operating policies and procedures.	_____
6. Delegates responsibility and authority when appropriate.	_____
7. Organizes and administers in a confident manner.	_____
8. Has skill in recruiting staff and students.	_____
9. Is a good manager of resources.	_____
10. Uses objective and fair methods of allocating resources.	_____
11. Acts fairly and decisively on important issues.	_____
12. Provides leadership.	_____
13. Uses good executive judgment.	_____
14. Keeps communication lines open.	_____
15. Is accessible to staff and students.	_____
16. Effectively uses personal contacts.	_____
17. Makes effective use of committees.	_____
18. Conducts effective staff meetings.	_____
19. Is effective in working with groups.	_____
20. Effectively uses memos, reports, and other contacts.	_____
21. Encourages individual initiative.	_____
22. Is fair in evaluations.	_____
23. Supports development of quality teaching.	_____

24. Supports development of quality research. _____

25. Supports quality institutional and public service. _____

PERSONAL TRAITS

1. Possesses high degree of integrity. _____

2. Is sensitive to student and staff concerns and needs. _____

3. Handles conflicts effectively. _____

4. Communicates ideas clearly. _____

5. Is an effective speaker. _____

6. Supportive of staff needs. _____

7. Displays an enthusiastic, positive outlook. _____

8. Treats faculty, staff, and students with respect and courtesy. _____

9. Supports the overall academic unit and the university. _____

PROFESSIONAL ACTIVITIES

1. Serves as a good representative to external publics. _____

2. Is active in professional organizations. _____

3. Represents an appropriate balance of administration, teaching, publication, professional, and public service. _____

4. Serves as a professional role model for staff. _____

OVERALL COMPETENCE/EXCELLENCE IN ROLE

COMMENTS (use back of page if necessary): _____

_____

_____

_____

_____

_____

_____

_____

_____

_____

_____

Index

Compiled by Linda Webster

JENNIFER CARGILL is Associate Director of Libraries for Information Access and Systems, Texas Tech University, Lubbock, TX. She is very active in librarianship and has written numerous books and articles on the subject, including *Librarian in Search of a Publisher: How to Get Published, Biographical Sources: A Guide to Dictionaries and Reference Works,* and *Keeping Track of What You Spend: The Librarian's Guide to Simple Bookkeeping.*

GISELA M. WEBB is Assistant Director of Libraries for Administrative Services, Texas Tech University, Lubbock, TX. She holds a master's degree in both Library Science and Public Administration.